Gulf ARABIC

Gulf Arabic is a variety of the Arabic language spoken in Eastern Arabia around the coasts of the Persian Gulf in Kuwait, Bahrain, Qatar, the United Arab Emirates, southern Iraq, eastern Saudi Arabia, northern Oman, and by some Iranian Arabs.

Dr.A.M.K. SIDDIQUI

H.No#12-2-825/7
Ansar complex, 2nd floor
Mehdipatnam, Hyderabad-500028
Tel. 9140-6514-6277, 9140-6634-6277
Email: info@jilt.co.in

Website : www.jilt.co.in

#8-3-4,Opp.Postoffice,Mettugadda,
Mahbubnagar-509001,India.
Tel.9188-8666-6156
Email: info@jilt.in

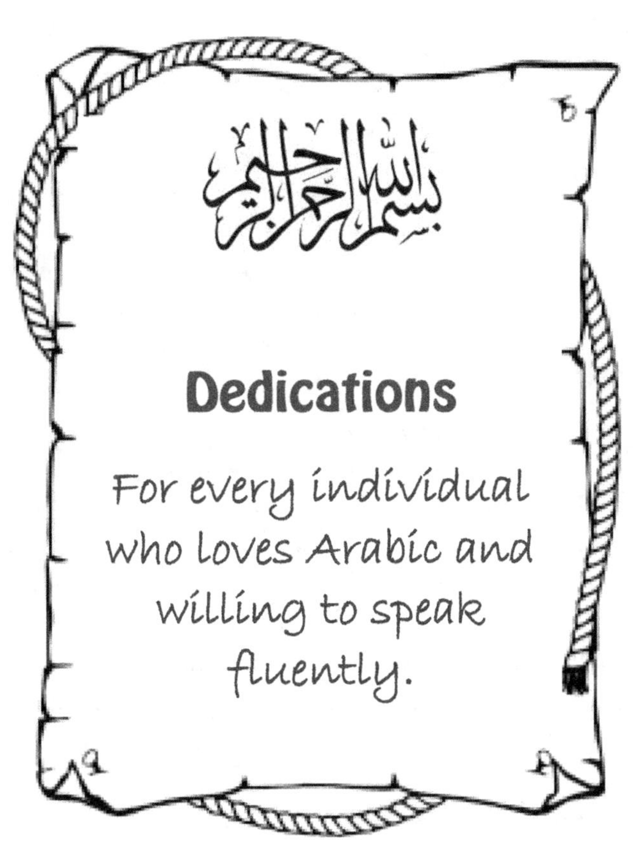

Dedications

For every individual
who loves Arabic and
willing to speak
fluently.

Contents

Preface

Arabic is one of the greatest and mighty language in the world. At the same time its grammar, morphology, rhetoric, vocabulary, syntax and phonetics are based on the key and important functions of language. Verily it is more scientific and intellectual language in the world. Indeed, vocabulary bank is most updated for all fields of study and research. Undoubtedly there is no other alternate for Arabic language in the world. It is the fourth widely spoken language in the world and official language of 25 countries.

After the recent crisis of 2007-08 all business magnets and giants are turning their attraction to the Arab lands, for its high business potential. Which is why there is a boom of wonderful opportunities and many prospect candidates are flocking to these dessert lands. Scope for Arabic language is getting higher and higher and almost all developed and developing countries' students are focusing and selecting it as a research subject in the universities and making it a successful source for employment.

This book is also an important tool to help and guide the students & learners with excellent colloquial Arabic conversations. All efforts have been made to make the curriculum more comprehensive and effective with numerous exercises for practices after every lesson. By which learners shall be able to understand and speak Arabic fluently.

At the end I'm very thankful to Mr.Abul Khair Siddiqui (CEO - JILT PVT.LTD) for continuing insistence and assistance for publishing this book with great focus and dynamic feedback, He has helped me a lot every time I needed, very proactively. In editing of this book I'm thankful to Dr.Mohd Junaid Zakir (Assistant Professor MANUU). And each and everybody who was focused on this elegant book , especially Mr.Abu Umar Siddiqui ,Mr. Mohd Nazeeruddin sahab Persident of ASREF , Best Friend Mr.Mohd Gazi Fahimheemudin, trusted students Mr. Syed Basharath Mehdi , Ms.Maryam al-avdhaly Yamani , and dear brother Abdul Raheem Siddiqui , and those who helped me to make this possible.

A.M.K. SIDDIQUI
Hyderabad - Deccan

Lesson-1
Introduction

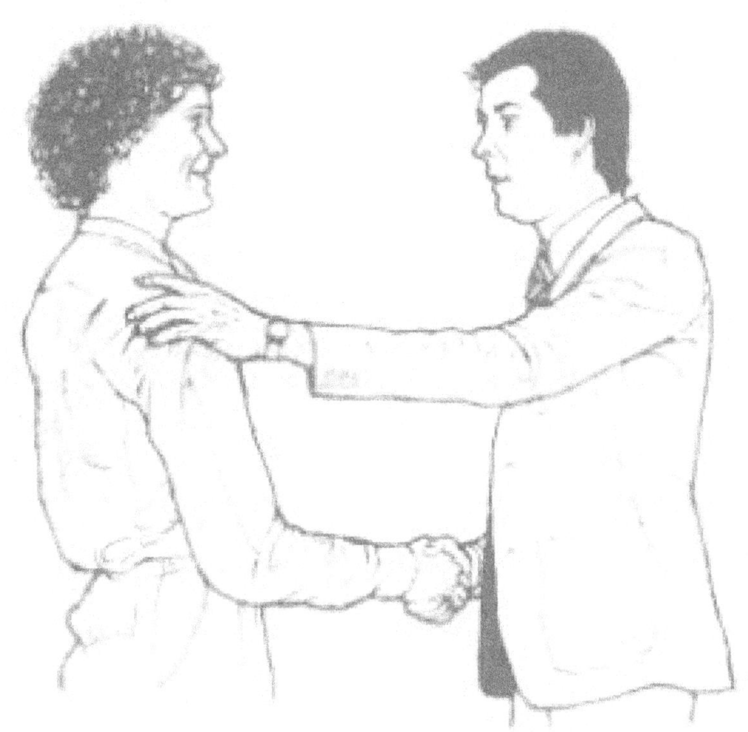

ENGLISH	ROMAN	ARABIC	S.No
My name is Khalid.	*Esmi- Khalid.*	إسمي خالد۔	١
What is your name?	*Shu-ismuk.*	شواسمك؟	٢
My name is Ahmed.	*Esmi-Ahmed.*	إسمي أحمد۔	٣
Where are you from?	*Min-ven-anta?*	من وين أنت؟	٤
I'm from Cairo.	*Ana –min-Al qahira.*	أنا من القاهرة۔	٥
And where are you from?	*Va-anta-min-ven?*	وأنت من وين؟	٦
I'm from Berut in Lebanon.	*Ana-min- Berut-fi- Libnan.*	أنا من بيروت فى لبنان۔	٧

التدريب – I

Answer the Following questions?

1 Shu Esmuk?

١   شو إسمك؟

2 Shu-Ismu - Abuk?

٢   شو إسم أبوك؟

3 Shu-Ismu - Ummuk?

٣   شو إسم أمك؟

4 Min - Ven - Anta?

٤   من وين أنت؟

التدريب – II

Match the Following Words From Arabic to English

S.No	Roman	Arabic	English
1	Esm	إسم	What
2	Ven	وين	Berut
3	Al qahira	القاهرة	Name
4	Berut	بيروت	Cairo
5	Shu	شو	Where

التدريب – III

Translate the Following Words in Arabic

S.No	English	Arabic
1	You	....
2	He	....
3	She	....
4	His	....
5	We	....

التدريب – IV

Translate the Following Words in English

English	Arabic	Roman	S.No
....	أنا	Ana	1
....	أنتم	Antum	2
....	أنت	Anti	3
....	ك	Ka	4
....	ها	Ha	5

Lesson-2
Self Introduction

ENGLISH	ROMAN	ARABIC	S.No
My name is Saleh.	*Esmi-Saleh.*	إسمى صالح۔	١
I'm from Sharjah.	*Ana-minash-Shariqah.*	أنا من الشارقة۔	٢
My name is Zainab.	*Esmi-Zainab.*	إسمى زينب۔	٣
I'm from Sanah in yemen.	*Ana-minSan-a fil-yaman.*	أنا من صنعاء فى اليمن۔	٤
Welcome how are you?	*Ahlan-wa-sahlan-shulunak?*	اهلاً وسهلاً شلونك؟	٥
I'm fine and what about you?	*Zain-wa-anti?*	زين وأنتِ؟	٦
I'm fine, thank you.	*Bikhair-mashkoor.*	بخير مشكور۔	٧

التدريب – I

Answer the Following questions?

1	Min-Ven-Saleh?	١ من وين صالح؟
2	Min-Ven-Zainab?	٢ من وين زينب؟
3	Man-Min-Ash-Sharqah?	٣ مَن مِن الشارقة؟
4	Shulunak?	٤ شلونك؟

التدريب – II

Match the Following Words From Arabic to English

S.No	Roman	Arabic	English
1	Sana'a	صنعاء	My Name
2	Al-yaman	اليمن	Sharja
3	Maskoor	مشكور	Sana'a
4	Shariqah	الشارقة	Thank you
5	Esmi	اسمى	Yaman

التدريب – III

Translate the Following Words in Arabic

S.No	English	Arabic
1	Fine	....
2	Thank you	....
3	I	....
4	From	....
5	You	....

التدريب – IV

Translate the Following Words in English

English	Arabic	Roman	S.No
....	أنتن	Antunnah	1
....	ك	Ka	2
....	كما	Kuma	3
....	كم	Kum	4
....	كن	Kunna	5

Lesson-3
Greetings

ENGLISH	ROMAN	ARABIC	S.No
Good evening.	*Massa-kalla-bil-khair.*	مساك الله بالخير۔	١
Good evening.	*Massa-kalla-bil-khair.*	مساك الله بالخير۔	٢
Welcome.	*Ahlan-wa-sahlan.*	اهلاً وسهلاً!	٣
How are you?	*Kaif-anti?*	كيف أنتِ؟	٤
I'm fine.	*Zainah-bikhair.*	زينة بخير۔	٥
And what about you?	*Va-anti?*	وأنتِ۔	٦
I'm fine.	*Zainah.*	زينة۔	٧
How is your family?	*Shulu-nal-ahl?*	شلون الاهل؟	٨
All are fine.	*Kullana-bikhair.*	كلنا بخير۔	٩
Good-bye.	*Ma- assalamah.*	مع السلامة۔	١٠

التدريب – I

Answer the Following questions?

1 Kaif- Aanta?	١ كيف أنت؟
2 Shulunal- Ahal?	٢ شلون الأهل؟
3 Min - Ven- Anta?	٣ من وين أنت؟
4 Shu- Esmu- Ummuk?	٤ شو إسم أمك؟

التدريب – II

Match the Following Words From Arabic to English

S.No	Roman	Arabic	English
1	Al- Ahal	الأهل	All
2	Ahlan Wa Sahlan	اهلاً وسهلاً	Family
3	Kulluna	كلنا	Good bye
4	Asalamah	السلامة	Fine
5	Bi Khair	بخير	Wel Come

التدريب – III

Translate the Following Words in Arabic

S.No	English	Arabic
1	Good bye	....
2	Fine	....
3	Wel Come	....
4	Good evening	....
5	Family	....

التدريب – IV

Translate the Following Words in English

English	Arabic	Roman	S.No
....	ها	Haa	1
....	ي	Iee	2
....	نا	Naa	3
....	نحن	Nahnu	4
....	من	Min	5

Lesson-4
About the work

ENGLISH	ROMAN	ARABIC	S.No
Zaid from Sana in yaman.	*Zaid-min-Sana-fi-Al-yaman.*	زيد من صنعاء فى اليمن-	١
He is a doctor in the hospital.	*Huva-daktor-fi-Al-mustashfah.*	هو دكتور فى المستشفى-	٢
I'm an engineer from Abu zahbi.	*Ana-muhandis-min-Abuzahbi.*	أنا مهندس من أبو ظبي-	٣
I'm working in the Ministry of Petroleum.	*Shugli-fi-wizaratil-betrol.*	شغلى فى وزارة البترول-	٤
My sister is secretary in Abu Dhahbi bank.	*Ukhti-sukritaira-fi-bank-abu-Zahbi.*	أختى سكرتيرة فى بنك أبو ظبي-	٥

التدريب – I

Answer the Following questions?

1	Zaid-min-ven?	١ زيد من وين ؟
2	Ven- ukhtuka- sukurterah?	٢ وين أختك سكريترة؟
3	Min- aina- al muhandis?	٣ من أين المهندس؟
4	Ven- zaid- shagal?	٤ وين زيد شغال؟

التدريب – II

Match the Following Words From Arabic to English

S.No	Roman	Arabic	English
1	Muhandis	مهندس	Yaman
2	Daktor	دكتور	Engineer
3	sukurterah	سكريترة	Secretary
4	Wizarat-Ul-Btrool	وزارة البترول	Doctor
5	Al-Yaman	اليمن	Ministry of Petroleum

التدريب – III

Translate the Following Words in Arabic

S.No	English	Arabic
1	Egypt	....
2	Ministry	....
3	Yaman	....
4	Rasul Khima	....
5	Doctor	....

التدريب – IV

Translate the Following Words in English

English	Arabic	Roman	S.No
....	فى	Fee	1
....	من	Min	2
....	على	A'la	3
....	الى	Ilaa'	4
....	مروحة	Mirwaha	5

Lesson-5
About others

ENGLISH	ROMAN	ARABIC	S.No
Good evening "o" Rashid.	*Massa-kalla-bil-khair-ya-Rashid*	مساك الله بالخير يا راشد	١
This is Salim.	*Haza-Salim*	هذا سالم ـ	٢
He is manager in a company here.	*Hua-mudeer-fi-shareeka-huna*	هو مدير في شركة هنا ـ	٣
And she is Wardha.	*Wa-hazihi-wardha*	وهذه وردة ـ	٤
She is a nurse in Qatar hospital.	*Hia-mumarrizah-fi-mustashfa-Qatar*	هي ممرضة في المستشفى قطر ـ	٥
They are from Saudia.	*Hum-min-al-saudiya*	هم من السعودية ـ	٦
Welcome where are you from in Saudia?	*Ahlan-wa-sahlan-antum-min-vain-fi-saudiya?*	اهلاً وسهلاً أنتم من وين في السعودية؟	٧
From Riyadh.	*Min-Al-Riyadh*	من الرياض ـ	٨
Are you from here? Yes I am here from Qatar.	*Wa-anta-min hina? ay-Ana-min-hina-min-Qatar*	وأنت من هنا؟ أي أنا من هنا من قطر ـ	٩

التدريب – I

Answer the Following questions?

1	Mon- Mudeer-Sharika?	١ من مدير الشركة؟
2	Mon- Al-Mumarrizah- Fil-Mustashfa?	٢ من الممرضة فى المستشفى؟
3	Min-Ven-Antum-Fi-Saudia?	٣ من وين أنتم فى السعودية؟
4	Min-Ven-Anta?	٤ من وين أنت؟

التدريب – II

Match the Following Words From Arabic to English

S.No	Roman	Arabic	English
1	Al-Mumarrizah	الممرضة	Qatar
2	Al-Mustashfa	المستشفى	The Nurse
3	Sharika	شركة	Manager
4	Mudeer	مدير	The Company
5	Qatar	قطر	The Hospital

التدريب – III

Translate the Following Words in Arabic

S.No	English	Arabic
1	Pharmacy	....
2	Madicine	....
3	Injection	....
4	Surgery	....
5	Hospital	....

التدريب – IV

Translate the Following Words in English

English	Arabic	Roman	S.No
....	سيارة	Siyyaerah	1
....	هذا	Haza	2
....	هذه	Hazihi	3
....	مكتب	Maktab	4
....	سبورة	Suboorah	5

Lesson-6
About Family

ENGLISH	ROMAN	ARABIC	S.No
My friend Hamid is an American	*Sadeeqi-hamid –amricani.*	صديقى حامدأمريكانى.	١
He is from Washington.	*Hua-min-madeena-washintan.*	هو من مدينة واشنطن.	٢
He is a manager in Shal company in Qatar.	*Hua-mudeer-fi-shareka-shal-fi-Qatar.*	هو مدير فى شركة شل فى قطر.	٣
Fatima wife of Hamid.	*Fatima-zojath-hamid.*	فاطمة زوجة حامد.	٤
She is an Egyptian.	*Hia-misriyah.*	هى مصرية.	٥
She is working as a nurse in Qatar Hospital.	*Shugluha-mumarrizah-fi-Al-mustashfa-fi-Qatar.*	شغلها ممرضة فى المستشفى فى قطر.	٦
Their daughter is Sara.	*Bintu-hum-Sara.*	بنتهم ساره.	٧
She is an employee in the bank.	*Movazifah-fil-bank.*	مؤظفة فى البنك.	٨
Their son's name is Salim.	*Waladu-hum-ismuhu-Salim.*	ولدهم إسمه سالم.	٩
He is a student in the school.	*Hua-talib-fil-Madrasah.*	هو طالب فى المدرسة.	١٠

التدريب – I

Answer the Following questions?

1 Shu- Esmu- Sadeequk? — ١ شو اسم صديقك؟

2 Min- Ven-Sadeequk? — ٢ من وين صديقك؟

3 Mon-Mudeer-Fisharikah-shill? — ٣ من مدير في شركة شل؟

4 Min-Ven-Fatima? — ٤ من وين فاطمة؟

التدريب – II

Match the Following Words From Arabic to English

S.No	Roman	Arabic	English
1	Sharikah	شركة	School
2	Mustashfa	المستشفى	Employee
3	Mudeer	المدير	Manager
4	Muwazzahfa	المؤظفة	Hospital
5	Madarsah	المدرسة	Company

التدريب – III

Translate the Following Words in Arabic

S.No	English	Arabic
1	Bank	....
2	Student	....
3	Americe	....
4	Name	....
5	Washington	....

التدريب – IV

Translate the Following Words in English

English	Arabic	Roman	S.No
....	فصل	Fasal	1
....	ثلاجة	Thalajah	2
....	جوّال	Jawwal	3
....	مهندس	Muhandis	4
....	مدرس	Mudarris	5

Lesson-7
Greetings

ENGLISH	ROMAN	ARABIC	S.No
Peace be upon you.	*Assalamu-alekum.*	السلام عليكم.	١
And also to you.	*Wa-lekum-assalam.*	وعليكم السلام.	٢
How are you?	*Kaifa-antih.?*	كيف أنتِ؟	٣
I'm really fine.	*Wallah-hi-zain.*	والله زين.	٤
And what about you?	*Wa-anti ?*	وأنتِ؟	٥
Fine!	*Tai-iba.*	طيبة.	٦
How is the family?	*Kaifal-a-e-lah?*	كيف العائلة؟	٧
You all are fine inshallah?	*Kullukum-bikhair-insha-Allah?*	كلكم بخير انشاء الله؟	٨
All of us are fine , thank you	*Kul-lu-na-bikhair-mashkur.*	كلنا بخير مشكور.	٩
In the safety of Allah	*Fi-ama-nil-Allah.*	فى أمان الله.	١٠

التدريب – I
Answer the Following questions?

Kaif-Anti? ١ كيف أنت؟

Kaif-Al-Aelah? ٢ كيف العائلة؟

Min-Ven-Fatimah? ٣ من وين فاطمة؟

Aina-Fatimah-Shagalah? ٤ أين فاطمة شغالة؟

التدريب – II
Match the Following Words From Arabic to English

S.No	Roman	Arabic	English
1	Aelah	العائلة	And also to you
2	Walad	ولد	Peace to upon you
3	Zain	زين	Fine
4	Assalamu Alekum	السلام عليكم	Family
5	Walekum Assalam	وعليكم السلام	Son

التدريب – III
Translate the Following Words in Arabic

S.No	English	Arabic
1	Insha-Allah	....
2	Fine	....
3	Family	....
4	Safety	....
5	How	....

التدريب – IV
Translate the Following Words in English

English	Arabic	Roman	S.No
....	رف	Ruf	1
....	حاسوب	Hasoob	2
....	طالب	Talib	3
....	صديق	Sadeeq	4
....	أخ	Akhun	5

Lesson-8
With The Manager

ENGLISH	ROMAN	ARABIC	S.No
Peace be upon you.	*Assalamu-alekum.*	السلام عليكم.	١
And same to you.	*Wa-alekum-assalam.*	وعليكم السلام.	٢
My name is Omar s/o Rashid.	*Ismi-Omar-bin-Rashed.*	إسمى عمر بن راشد.	٣
I have an appointment with Manager.	*Indi-maoid-ma-Al mudeer.*	عندى موعد مع المدير.	٤
O.k. come on Saturday.	*Zain-tafazzal-yo-mus-sabt.*	زين تفضل يوم السبت.	٥
I have an appointment with Manager today.	*Indi- maoid-ma- Al-mudeer-al-yom!*	عندى موعد مع المديراليوم.	٦
When? At what time?	*Mata? Ay-ye –sa-atah.?*	متى؟ أي الساعة؟	٧
12 '0' clock.	*Assa-atu-isnaashar.*	االساعة اثنا عشر.	٨
Is Manager here?	*Almudeer-hina?*	المديرهنا؟	٩
Oh Yeah!	*Ae-na-am.*	أى نعم.	١٠
Manager is here.	*Al-Mudeer-hina.*	المديرهنا!	١١
Welcome! Sit here.	*Ta-faz-zal- istarih.*	تفضل إسترح.	١٢

التدريب – I
Answer the Following questions?

1 Lman Mauid Ma' Al-Mudeer?   ١   لمن موعد مع المدير؟

2 Hal-Mudeer-Hina?   ٢   هل المدير هنا؟

3 Fi-Ayyi-Sa ah- Mauid Al-Muayim?   ٣   فى أى الساعة موعد المعين؟

4 Shu-Esmu-Waladu-Fatimah?   ٤   شو إسم ولد فاطمة؟

التدريب – II
Match the Following Words From Arabic to English

S.No	Roman	Arabic	English
1	Assaath	الساعة	Yes
2	Alyaom	اليوم	Time
3	Mauid	موعد	Come
4	Tafazzal	تفضل	Today
5	Naam	نعم	Appointement

التدريب – III
Translate the Following Words in Arabic

S.No	English	Arabic
1	Saturday	....
2	Time	....
3	12 'O' clock	....
4	Come	....
5	Week	....

التدريب – IV
Translate the Following Words in English

English	Arabic	Roman	S.No
....	صباح	Sabah	1
....	مساء	Masa	2
....	نهار	Nahaar	3
....	الخير	Al-khair	4
....	اسمى	Esmi	5

Lesson-9
With The Minister

ENGLISH	ROMAN	ARABIC	S.No
Good morning 'O' Laila! Welcome!	*Sabbaha kallah-bil-khair- ya-laila-ya-ahla-wa- marhaba*	صبحك الله بالخير يا ليلى، يا اهلا ومرحبا!	١
I have an appointment with minister at 1 'o' clock.	*Indi-maoid-ma-Al-wazeer- sa-atu-wahdah*	عندي موعد مع الوزير ساعة وحدة۔	٢
Minister is here?	*Al-wazeer-hina*	الوزير هنا؟	٣
Yes, he Is here	*Ay-ye-na-am-hina*	أي نعم، هنا۔	٤
He is doing some work now.	*Bas- mashgul -shu-yah-al- heen*	بس مشغول شوية الحين۔	٥
Come and take the seat.	*Tafazzali-istareehi*	تفضلي استريحي۔	٦
Thank you.	*Mash-korah*	مشكورة۔	٧
Take Coffee 'o' Qahmis!	*Qahwa-ya-Qamis!*	قهوة يا خميس!	٨

التدريب – I

Answer the Following questions?

1   Hal-Al-Wazir-Hina?   ١   هل الوزير هنا؟

2   Mn-Mashgool -Alheen?   ٢   من المشغول الحين؟

3   Mata-Al- Mauid -Ma-Alwazir?   ٣   متى الموعد مع الوزير؟

4   Shulunal-Ahal?   ٤   شلون الأهل؟

التدريب – II

Match the Following Words From Arabic to English

S.No	Roman	Arabic	English
1	Mashgool	مشغول	I' have
2	Alwazir	الوزير	Busy
3	Mauid	موعد	Now
4	Alheen	الحين	Minister
5	Endi	عندى	Appointement

التدريب – III

Translate the Following Words in Arabic

S.No	English	Arabic
1	1 'o' Clock	....
2	Coffee	....
3	Thank you	....
4	Come	....
5	Have a Seat	....

التدريب – IV

Translate the Following Words in English

English	Arabic	Roman	S.No
....	شو	Shu	1
....	موعد	Mauid	2
....	تفضل	Tafazzal	3
....	نعم	Naam	4
....	الحين	Al-heen	5

Lesson-10
About Family

ENGLISH	ROMAN	ARABIC	S.No
My name is Abdullah.	*Esmi-Abdullah*	إسمى عبدالله.	١
I'm from Bahrain.	*Ana-minAl-bahrain*	أنا من البحرين.	٢
I'm married ,I have a son & a daughter	*Ana-mutazavvig-wa-indi-walad-wabint*	أنا متزوج وعندى ولد وبنت.	٣
The son's name is Saad and the daughter's name is Saleha.	*Alwalad-Esmuhu-Saad-walbint-Esmuha-Saliha*	الولد إسمه سعد والبنت إسمها صالحة.	٤
They are studying in school.	*Hum-fil-madrasah*	هم فى المدرسة.	٥
I'm working in the Ministry of Health.	*Ana-shugly-fi-vizaratis-sih-ha*	أنا شغلى فى وزارةالصحة.	٦
Weather in Behran is good in winter.	*Alhawa-filBehrain-vajid-zain-fil-shita-*	الهوا فى البحرين واجدزين فى الشتاء.	٧
Neither hot nor cold.	*Mahowa-bihar-wama-howa-bibarid*	ماهو بحار وماهو ببارد.	٨
But in Kair it is hot and humid.	*Wa-lakin-fi-Ai-kair-alhawa-har-wa-rutb*	ولكن فى الكيرالهوا حار ورطب.	٩

التدريب – I
Answer the Following questions?

1	Min-Ven-Abduallah?	من وين عبدالله؟ ١
2	Shu-Esmu-Walad- Abduallah?	شو إسم ولد عبدالله؟ ٢
3	Shu-Ismu-Bint- Abduallah?	شو إسم بنت عبدالله؟ ٣
4	Ayyna- Abduallah-Shaggal?	أين عبدالله شغال؟ ٤

التدريب – II
Match the Following Words From Arabic to English

S.No	Roman	Arabic	English
1	Mutazavvij	متزوج	Hot
2	Almadarsa	المدرسة	Married
3	Wajid	واجد	School
4	Haar	حار	Cold
5	Barid	بارد	Avaliable

التدريب – III
Translate the Following Words in Arabic

S.No	English	Arabic
1	Son	....
2	Daughter	....
3	Ministry of health	....
4	Hot	....
5	Cold	....

التدريب – IV
Translate the Following Words in English

English	Arabic	Roman	S.No
....	الصحة	As-sihhah	1
....	الممرضة	Al-Mumarrizah	2
....	الطبيب	At-Tabeeb	3
....	المشتشفى	Al-Mustashfa	4
....	الضابط	Al-Zaabitu	5

Lesson-11
Climate

ENGLISH	ROMAN	ARABIC	S.No
Peace be upon you.	*Assalamu-alekum*	السلام عليكم۔	١
Same to you.	*Wa-alekum-assalam*	وعليكم السلام۔	٢
What is your name?	*Shant-ismuk?*	شنة اسمك؟	٣
My name is Aslam.	*Esmi-Aslam*	إسمى أسلم۔	٤
How are you?	*Kaifa-haaluk?*	كيف حالك؟	٥
Fine, praise be to Allah.	*Tayyib-alhamdu-lillah*	طيب الحمد الله۔	٦
Where are you from?	*Anta-min-wain?*	أنت من وين۔	٧
I'm from America.	*Ana-min-America*	أنا من امريكا۔	٨
Where in America?	*Min-vain-fee-America?*	من وين فى أمريكا؟	٩
From toosan in Arizona.	*Min-Toosan-fil-Razonah*	من توسان فى الرزونة ۔	١٠
You speak Arabic very	*Antah-tatakallam-Arabi-*	أنت تتكلم عربى زين والله۔	١١

well!	*zain-wallah*	
▪ Not so good, I speak a little bit Arabic.	▪ *La-ma huwa-bizain-ana- Atakallam- shuya-arabi*	لا ماهو بزين أنا أتكلم شوى عربى۔ ١٢
▪ How is climate in Toosan in winter?	▪ *Kaifa-al-taqash-fi-Toosan- fis-shitaa*	كيف الطقس فى التوسان فى الشتاء۔ ١٣
▪ There is cold and nice in winter.	▪ *Barid-wa-zain-fis-shitaa*	بارد وزين فى الشتاء۔ ١٤
▪ In Kair the climate is hot at every time.	▪ *Fil-kair-Alhawa-haar?-Ay- wallah, kullush-har.*	فى الكير الهوا حار؟ أي والله كلش حار۔ ١٥

التدريب – I

Answer the Following questions?

1	Shanat-Esmuk?	١ شنة اسمك؟
2	Kaif-Halak?	٢ كيف حالك؟
3	Hal-Anta-Tatakallam-Arabi?	٣ هل أنت تتكلم عربى؟
4	Min-Ven-Fi-America?	٤ من وين فى امريكة؟

التدريب – II

Match the Following Words From Arabic to English

S.No	Roman	Arabic	English
1	Esm	الاسم	Arizona
2	Al-shita	الشتاء	Fine
3	Tayyib	الطيب	Name
4	Al-rizona	الرزونة	America
5	America	امريكة	Winter

التدريب – III

Translate the Following Words in Arabic

S.No	English	Arabic
1	Praise be to Allah	....
2	Speak	....
3	How are you	....
4	From	....
5	Peace be upon you	....

التدريب – IV

Translate the Following Words in English

English	Arabic	Roman	S.No
....	الهند	Al-hind	1
....	الصين	As-seen	2
....	يابان	Yaban	3
....	باكستان	Bakistan	4
....	القاهرة	Al-qahirah	5

Lesson-12
Taxi

ENGLISH	ROMAN	ARABIC	S.No
Taxi.	*Taksi.*	تيكسى-	١
Would you like to go?	*Wa-anta-bitaruh?*	وأنت بتروح؟	٢
I want to go to Haltom Hotel.	*Abi-Arooho-hotal–Al-hiltam.*	أبي أروح اوتيل الهلتم-	٣
How much you want?	*Kam-tureed?*	كم تريد؟	٤
Twenty Dirham.	*Ishreen-Dirham.*	عشرين درهم-	٥
Twenty Dirham is too much!	*Ishreen- dirham- haza-kaseer.*	عشرين درهم هذا كثير!	٦
I will pay only 15Dirham.	*Adfav-qamsa-ashra-Dirham.bas.*	أدفع 15 درهم بس-	٧
Ok, Please have a seat.	*Zain-tafazzal.*	زين تفضل-	٨
Take this These are TwentyDirhams.	*Tafazzal-haza-ishreen-Dirham.*	تفضل هذا 20 درهم-	٩
And give me the balance five Dirhams.	*Tafazzal-albaqi-qamsa-Dirahim.*	تفضل البا قى5 دراهم-	١٠
Thank you, May protect you Allah.	*Mashkoor-fi-ama-nillah.*	مشكور فى اما ن الله -	١١
Good bye!	*Ma-assalamah.*	مع السلا مة-	١٢
I want to go to the Ministry of Training.	*Ureed-arooh-vizarat-al tarbi-yah.*	أريد أروح وزارة التربية -	١٣

English	Transliteration	Arabic	
Ok, Please come.	*Zain-tafazzal.*	زين تفضل ـ	١٤
How much would you charge?	*Kam-tabi?*	كم تبي؟	١٥
20Dirhams.	*Eshroon-Dirham.*	20درهم ـ	١٦
Government rate ok, Are you from Qatar, no I am from Saudi	*Sarul-hokomah-zain, anta – min-Qatar, la, min-as-Saudia.*	سعر الحكومة ، زين ، أنت من قطر ، لا من السعودية ـ	١٧
Is this first time to Doha, No it is third time	*Hazihi-Avwaul-mar-ah fil-duha-, la-hazihee-salis-mar-ah.*	هذه اول مرة فى الدوحة ،لا هذه ثالث مرة ـ	١٨
From how many years?	*Kam-sara-laka-hena.*	كم صارلك هنا ـ	١٩
From a period, about 10 year.	*Min-zamaan, sara-li-ashra-seneen.*	من زمان، صارلي عشر سنين ـ	٢٠
Where are you working?	*Wain-tashtagl?*	وين تشغل؟	٢١
I am working in the ministry of Training.	*Fi-vizaratil-tar-bi-ah.*	فى وزارة التربية .	٢٢
May be you feel well here in Doha.	*Insha-Allah-Ajabatka-Doha?*	إنشاء الله عجبتك الدوحة؟	٢٣
Yes sure.	*Ayyi-aajabatni-wajed.*	أى ، أعجبتنى واجد ـ	٢٤
I felt good with everything here;	*Ana-kullush-mustanis-hena.*	أنا كلش مستانس هنا ـ	٢٥

التدريب – I

Answer the Following questions?

1	Ven-Anta-Bi-Tarooh?	وين أنت بتروح؟	١
2	Kam-Tureed-Al-Fuloos?	كم تريد الفلوس؟	٢
3	Ven-Tashgul?	وين تشغل؟	٣
4	Hal-Anta-Min-Qatar?	هل أنت من قطر؟	٤

التدريب – II

Match the Following Words From Arabic to English

S.No	Roman	Arabic	English
1	Mustanis	مستأنس	First time
2	Dirham	درهم	Good
3	Kaseer	كثير	Dirham
4	Zamaan	زمان	Too much
5	Awwalu Marrah	أول مرة	Period

التدريب – III

Translate the Following Words in Arabic

S.No	English	Arabic
1	Ministry of Training	....
2	20 Dirhams	....
3	10 Years	....
4	Third time	....
5	Government rate	....

التدريب – IV

Translate the Following Words in English

English	Arabic	Roman	S.No
....	مشكور	Mashkoor	1
....	السلامة	Assalamah	2
....	واجد	Wajid	3
....	كم	Kam	4
....	تبى	Tabi	5

Lesson-13
About The Health

ENGLISH	ROMAN	ARABIC	S.No
Good morning 'O' Zubair .	*Sabbaha-kallah-bil-khair,ya-Zubair*	صبحک الله بالخير یا زبیر۔	١
Welcome, please come, have a seat .	*Ahlan-wa-sahlan, tafazzal-Istareeh .*	أهلاً وسهلاً ، تفضل إسترح۔	٢
Thank you .	*Mashkoor .*	مشكور۔	٣
Do You want tea?	*Tashrib-sha-ee*	تشرب شاي۔	٤
Would you like to drink tea or coffee?	*Tashrib-sha-e-aw-qahwah*	تشرب شاي أو قهوة۔	٥
Tea, cold tea…	*Wa-la- ayyi-shain-Baarid*	ولا اى شى بارد۔	٦
Tea, please.	*Sha-ee min-fazlik*	شاي من فضلک۔	٧
How are you and your family?	*Kaifa-haluk- kaifa-al-ahl?*	كيف حالک-كيف الأهل؟	٨
Really I am not fine today, I am sick so much.	*Wallah-mareez-al-yom-wallah-mariz-musaqan*	والله مريض اليوم والله مريض مسخن۔	٩
Go to the doctor.	*Roh-indad-daktoor*	روح عند الدكتور۔	١٠
I have an appointment with doctor today.	*Alyom-indi-maoid-ma-all-daktoor*	اليوم عندى موعد مع الدكتور۔	١١
With doctor Sami at 2:15, after Zuhar	*Ma'ad-daktoor-Sami-as-sa'ah-ethnain-al-arba'aqb-Al-zuhar*	مع الدكتور سامي الساعة إثنين الأربع عقب الظهر۔	١٢

التدريب – I

Answer the Following questions?

1	Kaaf-Halak? Wa Kaaf-Alahal?	كيف حالك؟ وكيف الأهل؟ ١
2	Hal laka-Moued-Maa-Daktoor Al-Youm?	هل لك موعد مع الدكتور اليوم؟ ٢
3	Shu-Ismu-Daktoor?	شو إسم الدكتور؟ ٣
4	Fi-Ayyi-Saa'ah-lakal-moueed-maal-Daktoor?	فى أي الساعة لك الموعد مع الدكتور؟ ٤

التدريب – II

Match the Following Words From Arabic to English

S.No	Roman	Arabic	English
1	Mariz	مريض	Cold
2	Musakhan	مسخن	Tea
3	Qahwah	قهوة	Sick
4	Shaiya	شاي	Coffee
5	Barid	بارد	So much

التدريب – III

Translate the Following Words in Arabic

S.No	English	Arabic
1	Thank you	....
2	Please	....
3	Have a seat	....
4	Go	....
5	Please Come	....

التدريب – IV

Translate the Following Words in English

English	Arabic	Roman	S.No
....	عقب	Aaqab	1
....	عندي	Indi	2
....	يا	Yaa	3
....	اليوم	Al-Youm	4
....	كيف	Kaifa	5

Lesson-14
Vegetable Market

ENGLISH	ROMAN	ARABIC	S.No
What is the price of tomato today?	*Kamit-tamatim-al-yom?*	كم الطماطم اليوم؟	١
10 Dirham 1KG.	*Ashra-Dirham-kilo.*	عشردرهم الكيلو۔	٢
It's too much expensive.	*Gaali-kaseer!*	غالى كثير!	٣
No it is not expensive.	*La-ma-huwa-bigali.*	لا ماهو بغالى۔	٤
Today in the market tomato is not available.	*Alyom-mafi-tamatim-wajid-fis-soq.*	اليوم مافى طماطم واجد فى السوق۔	٥
I'll pay you eight Dirham only.	*Adfa –samaniya-Dirham-bas.*	أدفع ثمانيه درهم بس؟	٦
No, it is less.	*Laa-haza-khaleel.*	لا ، هذا قليل!	٧
Ok then see you!	*Zain-fi-amani-allah.*	زين فى مان الله۔	٨

English	Transliteration	Arabic
Come.	Ta-aali.	٩ تعالى۔
Pay nine Dirham.	Tisa-Dirham.	١٠ تسع درهم۔
No only eight Dirhams	La-samaniya-dirham-bas.	١١ لا ثمانيه درهم بس۔
(even) I want to purchase eggs & oranges after that.	urid-ashtari-baiz-wa-burtoqal-bad.	١٢ أريد أشترى بيض وبرتقال بعد۔
Ok how much you want to purchase?	Zain-kam-tab-een.?	١٣ زين كم تبين ؟
Give me three kilos of tomato's and 12 eggs and 24 oranges.	A-tini-salas-kilo-tamatam-wa-darzan-baiz-wa-darzanain-burtuqal.	١٤ أعطنى ثلاثة كيلو طماطم ودرزن بيض ودرزنين برتقال۔

التدريب – I

Answer the Following questions?

١ كم الطماطم اليوم؟

1 Kaam-attamatim-al-youm?

٢ كم تدفع درهم؟

2 Kam-tadfah-dirham?

٣ كم تريد بيض وبرتقال؟

3 Kam-tareed-baiz-wa-burtuqaal?

٤ هل أنت مريض اليوم؟

4 Hal-anta-mareez-al-youm?

التدريب – II

Match the Following Words From Arabic to English

S.No	Roman	Arabic	Nos	English	S.No
1	Baiz	بيض		Expensive	1
2	Burtuqaal	برتقال		Tomato	2
3	Tamatim	طماطم		Oranges	3
4	Samaniyah	ثمانية		Eggs	4
5	Gaali	غالى		Eight	5

التدريب – III

Translate the Following Words in Arabic

S.No	English	Arabic
1	Dirham	....
2	Dorzen	....
3	Nine Dirham	....
4	Market	....
5	Expensive	....

التدريب – IV

Translate the Following Words in English

English	Arabic	Roman	S.No
....	هذا	Haza	1
....	قليل	Qaleel	2
....	كثير	Kaseer	3
....	التفاح	At-Tuffah	4
....	فى	Fi	5

Lesson-15
Cooking

ENGLISH	ROMAN	ARABIC	S.No
Saliha wants to go to the market .	*Saliha-tab-i- taruhus-suq.*	صالحة تبيى تروح السوق۔	١
Because she wants to buy food, okra, black brinjal and green chilies.	*Li-an-naha-torid-tashtari-ta'am-wa-bamia-wa-bazinjan-aswad-wa-filfil-akhzar.*	لأنها تريد تشترى طعام وبامية و باذنجان أسود وفلفل أخضر۔	٢
tomorrow they have a party at home .	*Bakir-indahum-haflah-fil-bait.*	باكرعندهم حفلة فى البيت۔	٣
At 9 o'clock at night.	*Fis-sa'ah-tisa-fil-lail.*	فى الساعة تسع فى الليل۔	٤
Saliha want to cook the Arabian dish.	*Saliha-tabi- tathbakhi-akal-Arabi?*	صالحة تبي تطبخ أكل عربى۔	٥

• After that, she wants to purchase the meat, red Lebanese apples.	• *Bad-tureed-tashtari-laham-wa-tuffah-labnani- Ahmar*	٦ بعد تريد تشترى لحم وتفاح لبنانى أحمر.
• May be she will not get good meat today.	• *Yomkin-ma-tahsol-laham-zain-al-yom*	٧ يمكن ماتحصل لحم زين اليوم.
• She can purchase the meat tomorrow.	• *Hiya-taqdir-tashtari-laham-bakir*	٨ هى تقدر تشترى لحم باكر.
• Shaikha is the friend of Saliha	• *Shaikha-sadeeqah-Saliha*	٩ شيخة صديقة صالحة.
• Do you want to come to the house of Saliha and eat with her?	• *A-tureedu-tejee-bait-Saliha-wa-takul-wiyyahum*	١٠ أتريد تيجي بيت صالحة وتأكل وياهم.

التدريب – I

Answer the Following questions?

1 Hal- Saleha-Tarooh-As-Sooq?   ١ هل صالحة تروح السوق؟

2 Shu-Esmu-Sadiqatu-Saleha?   ٢ شوإسم صديقة صالحة؟

3 Fi-Ayyi-Saa'at-Haflah-Al-Youm?   ٣ فى أي الساعة حفلة اليوم؟

4 Liman-Al-Haflah-Al-Youm?   ٤ لمن الحفلة اليوم؟

التدريب – II

Match the Following Words From Arabic to English

S.No	Roman	Arabic	English
1	Haflah	حفلة	Mutton
2	Tufah	تفاح	House
3	Al-bait	البيت	Party
4	Al-suqh	السوق	Apple
5	Laham	لحم	Market

التدريب – III

Translate the Following Words in Arabic

S.No	English	Arabic
1	Arabiyan Dish	....
2	Black brinjal	....
3	Green Chillies	....
4	Okra	....
5	Tommarrow	....

التدريب – IV

Translate the Following Words in English

English	Arabic	Roman	S.No
....	أحمر	Ahmar	1
....	الليل	Allail	2
....	أخضر	Akhzar	3
....	عندهم	Indahum	4
....	طماطم	Tamatim	5

Lesson-16
About Us

ENGLISH	ROMAN	ARABIC	S.No
Are you Jasim? Somebody is looking up for you.	*Hal-Anta-jasim? yurid-yashu-fak.*	هل أنت جاسم ؟ واحد يريد-*Wahid* يشوفك!	١
Ok Insha'Allah	*Khair-insha-allah.*	خير انشاء الله ۔	٢
By Allah, I am so busy I have some work	*Wa-allah-indi-shagal-wajid.*	والله عندى شغل واجد ۔	٣
I go to work at 6 o' clock in the morning and I will be back at 3 o'clock every day	*Arooh-ushgul-as-sabaah-as-saa-sittah-wa saa'ahsalasa-kulla-youm.*	أروح الشغل الصباح الساعة السادسة وأرجع ساعة ثلاث-*arji-o* كل يوم۔	٤
How is your family & relatives?	*Kaifal-aailah-wal-ayaal?*	كيف العائلة والعيال؟	٥
Nothing to be worried, everything is fine, tomorrow the school will open.	*La-bas-zain, bakir-tufta-hul-madrasa.*	لابأس زين ، باكر تفتح المدرسة ۔	٦

٧	والحين أروح البنك لأنني أريد أسحب فلوس۔	*Wal-heen-arroh-albank-liannani-orid-ashabu-fuls.*
	And now, I'll go to the bank because I need to withdraw some money.	
٨	الأولاد يردون الكتب والدفاتر والأقلام۔	*Al-aolaad-ureedunal-kutub-waldafatir-walaqlaam.*
	The children need text books, note books & pens.	
٩	المدرسة بعيدة؟	*Almadrasah-baeedah.*
	Is the school far?	
١٠	لا ، قريبة ، هم يمشون ، مرات *hum-*yroحون بالسيارة ومرات يروحون بالباص۔	*Laa-qareebah, yamshoon'mar-raat-yaruhun, bissayarah-wamar-raat-yaruhun-bilbaas.*
	No, it's near sometimes they go by walk, and sometime by car & some time by bus.	

التدريب – I

Answer the Following questions?

1 Mon-Shagal-Va-fi-Ayyi-Amal?

١   من الشغّال و فى أي عمل؟

2 Fi-Ayyi-Saa'ah-Anta-Tarooh-Al-Shugal?

٢   فى أي الساعة أنت تروح الشغل؟

3 Fi-Ayyi-Saa'-Targiu-Minash-Shugul?

٣   فى اي الساعة ترجع من الشغل؟

4 Mon-Yarooh-Al-Bank?

٤   من يروح البنك؟

التدريب – II

Match the Following Words From Arabic to English

S.No	Roman	Arabic	English
1	Al-Ayaal	العيال	Books
2	Al-Bank	البنک	Note books
3	Dafatir	دفاتر	Pens
4	Aqlam	أقلام	Bank
5	kutub	الكتب	Relatives

التدريب – III

Translate the Following Words in Arabic

S.No	English	Arabic
1	Withdraw	....
2	Money	....
3	Car	....
4	Bus	....
5	Near	....

التدريب – IV

Translate the Following Words in English

English	Arabic	Roman	S.No
....	لابأس	La-Baas	1
....	تفتح	Taftah	2
....	البنک	Al-Bank	3
....	الدفاتر	Al-Dafatir	4
....	الأولاد	Al-Aulad	5

Lesson-17
At The Petrol Pump

ENGLISH	ROMAN	ARABIC	S.No
Petrol pump /a petrol station.	*Mahattatul-Banzeen.*	محطة البنزين-	١
Normal or powered petrol, normal please.?	*Aadiyo-wala-Mumtaaz, aadi-minfazlik?*	عادي ولاممتاز، عادى من فضلك ؟	٢
How many liters you want?	*Kam-liter-tabi?*	كم لترتبي؟	٣
Make the tank full.	*Utrusih-tanki.*	أطرس التانكي-	٤
Insha'Allah.	*Insha'Allah.*	إن شاء الله-	٥
Please clean the jam parts, everything is dirty.	*Nazzef –fil-jam-min-fazlik, kullu-shai-wasakh.*	نظف الجام من فضلك ، كل الشى وسخ-	٦
Check the tyres.?	*Cheeki-at-tairaat.?*	شيک الطائرات؟	٧
Insha'Allah.	*Insha'Allah.*	إن شاء الله-	٨
Tyres are good.	*Al-tairaat-kullu-shaizain.*	الطائرات كل الشى زين-	٩
Check radiator and oil.	*Cheek-alrayadeetar,waz-*	شيک الرايديتر، والزيت-	١٠

	zait.		
■ Insha'Allah.	■ *Insha'Allah.*	إن شاء الله۔	۱۱
■ Radiator needs some water.	■ *Ra-yadeetar-yahtaaj-shovai-ma.*	رايديتر يحتاج شوي ماي۔	۱۲
■ The oil is less.	■ *Alzait-Qaleel.*	الزيت قليل۔	۱۳
■ It needs to be (filled) with powered oil.	■ *Tahtaj-quuti-zait.*	تحتاج قوتى زيت۔	۱٤
■ How much?	■ *Kam-yaseer?*	كم يصير؟	۱٥
■ One Dinar and 800 fills.	■ *Deenar-wasamaniah-miata-fils.*	دينار وثمانية مائة فلس۔	۱٦
■ This is one & half Deenar.	■ *Haaza-deenar-wanisf.*	هذا دينارو نصف۔	۱۷
■ Rest of the amount is tip for you.	■ *Albaqeelak-baqshish.*	الباقى لك بخشيش۔	۱۸
■ Thank you!	■ *Mashkoor.*	مشكور۔	۱۹

التدريب – I

Answer the Following questions?

1	Kam-litar-tabi?	١	كم ليتر تبى؟
2	Hal-taeeraat-kullu-shai-zain?	٢	هل الطائرات كلُ شئى زين؟
3	Kam-dinar-tahtaj?	٣	كم دينار تحتاج؟
4	Hal-radiatar-yahtaj-shuya-maa?	٤	هل رايدييتر يحتاج شوة ماء؟

التدريب – II

Match the Following Words From Arabic to English

S.No	Roman	Arabic	English
1	Attaierath	الطائرات	Tank
2	Radiatar	رايدييتر	Some
3	jaam	جام	Tyres
4	tanki	تانكى	Radiator
5	Shuya	شويه	Jam

التدريب – III

Translate the Following Words in Arabic

S.No	English	Arabic
1	Dirty	....
2	Powered	....
3	Normal	....
4	Tip	....
5	Petrol pump	....

التدريب – IV

Translate the Following Words in English

English	Arabic	Roman	S.No
....	نظف	Nazzif	1
....	السيارة	Al-sayayarah	2
....	المحطة	Al-mahattah	3
....	يحتاج	Yahtaj	4
....	محطة البنزين	Mahattatul Benzeen	5

Lesson-18
Meeting

ENGLISH	ROMAN	ARABIC	S.No
Good morning o' saeed!	*Sabbaha-kallah-bil-khair-ya-Saeed!*	صبحك الله بالخير يا سعيد!	١
Good morning! Where is your Car today?	*Sabbahal-khair-waish-fi-sayya-ratik-Al- yawm?*	صباح الخير ويش فى سيارتك اليوم؟	٢
The light is not working	*Al-lait-haqaha-mahua-be-zain.*	اليت حقها ماهو بزين ـ	٣
May be the light is no working.	*Yumkinul-misbha-ma-huwa-bizain.*	يمكن المصباح ما هو بزين ـ	٤
May Allah have peace upon you, in this week the light was not working	*Allahu-yusallimuk, allait-sara-lahu-usbooi-wa-huwa-ma-bizain.*	الله يسلمك، اليت صارله اسبوع وهو ما بزين ـ	٥
I don't know what was the problem	*Ma-adri-shu-mushkilah.*	ما ادرى شوالمشكلة ـ	٦
Ok, let it be.	*Zain-khallini-ashfah.*	زين خلنى أشفه ـ	٧
Are you coming tomorrow?	*Teji-bakir.*	تجى باكر؟	٨
May Allah have peace be upon, tomorrow its Friday ….holiday	*Allahu-yusallimuk-bakiral-jumah-utlath.*	الله يسلمك باكر الجمعةعطلة ـ	٩
come day after tomorrow	*Taal-aqb-bakir.*	تعال عقب باكر ـ	١٠

التدريب – I

Answer the Following questions?

1	Waish-Siyaratuka-Al-Youm?	١ ويش سيارتک اليوم؟
2	Haal-Tiji-Bakir?	٢ هل تجى باكر؟
3	Hal-Tadri-Ma- Mushkilah?	٣ هل تدرى ما المشكة؟
4	Hal-li-Youm-Al-Jummah-uotlah?	٤ هل لِيوم الجمة عطلة؟

التدريب – II

Match the Following Words From Arabic to English

S.No	Roman	Arabic	English
1	Al-Jummah	الجمعة	Light
2	Al-Musshkilah	المشكلة	Car
3	Bakir	باكر	Problem
4	Saiyyarh	سيارة	Tomorrow
5	Al-Baith	البيت	Friday

التدريب – III

Translate the Following Words in Arabic

S.No	English	Arabic
1	Holiday	....
2	Tomorrow	....
3	Come	....
4	Light	....
5	Week	....

التدريب – IV

Translate the Following Words in English

English	Arabic	Roman	S.No
....	المصباح	Al-Misbah	1
....	ما ادرى	Ma Adri	2
....	تعال	Ta'aal	3
....	عقب	Aqab	4
....	هاتف	Haatif	5

Lesson-19
Education

ENGLISH	ROMAN	ARABIC	S.No
I am Bahrainian from Manama.	*Ana-bahrini-minal-mana-mah*	أنا بحرينى من المنامة۔	١
I studied English two years in Darul muallimeen.	*Darustul-injiliziyyah-fi-daril-mu-allimina-sanatain-*	درست الإنجليزية فى دارالمعلمين سنتين۔	٢
I got the certificate last year	*Hasaltush-shahadah-al-aamal-mazi-*	حصلتُ الشهادة العام الماضى۔	٣
I am married alhamdu-lillah.	*Ana-mutazawwij-alhamdu-lillah-*	أنامتزوج الحمد لله۔	٤
I got the work as a teacher in Abu Dhabi.	*Hasaltu-wazifah-mu'allim-fi Abu-zahbi-*	حصلت وظيفة معلم فى أبو ظبى۔	٥
I could not visit Abu Dhabi for a long time.	*Ana-ma-ruhtu-bo-zahabi-min-zaman-*	أنا ماروحت أبو ظبى من زمان۔	٦
I and my wife went to the airport.	*Ruhna-ana-wa-hurmati-almatar-*	روحنا أنا وحرمتى المطار۔	٧
I paid for tickets.	*Dafatu-samanat-tazakir-*	دفعت ثمن التذاكر۔	٨
I paid almost 20 Bahraini Dinar for extra weight and	*Dafatu-taqreeban-ishreena-dinaran-bahreeni!haqiz-*	دفعت تقريبا عشرين دينار بحرينى حق الزيادة فى	٩

English	Transliteration	Arabic
two Dinar for airport tax.	ziyadah,fil-vazan-wa-dinarain-zareebah! haqil-matar-	الوزن ودينارين ضريبة حق المطار۔
■ We left the airport and reached Abu Dhabi just after half an hour.	■ Taraknal-matara-wa-wasalna-bu-zahbi-aqba-nisf-sa'ah۔	١٠ تركنا المطار ووصلنا أبوظبى عقب نصف ساعة۔
■ May Allah have peace be upon you, Abu Dhabi is near from Bahrain.	■ Abu-zahbi-allahu-yusallimuk-qaribah-minal-Behrain.	١١ أبو ظبى الله يسلمك قريبة من البحرين۔
■ I have a friend in Abu Dhabi	■ Indi-rafique-fi-abuzahbi.	١٢ عندى رفيق فى أبوظبى۔
■ We lived with him & his family for one month.	■ Sakanna-wiyah, wiyah-aailatah-shahar-wahid.	١٣ سكنا وياه، وياه عائلته شهر واحد۔
■ After that we got the house from government.	■ Wabadian-hasalna-bait-minal-hukoomah.	١٤ وبعدين حصلنا بيت من الحكومة ۔
■ There is everything available in the house, i.e. fridge, washing machine, chairs & bed sheets.	■ Walbait-fehi-kulu-shaiyi-sallajah-wagassalah-wakanbat-wa-karas-wa-kafayath.	١٥ والبيت فيه كل شئ ثلاجة وغسالة و كنبات وكراسي و كرفيات۔
■ The house is small but we don't want a big house.	■ Albeit-sageer-walakinna-ma-nabee-kabeer.	١٦ البيت صغير ولكننا مانبى كبير۔
■ Because we don't have a family and children with us who would be here.	■ Li-anna-ma-indana-ayaal-wa-ahl-una-ma yaskunoon-ma'ana.	١٧ لأن ما عند نا عيال وأهلنا ما يسكنون معنا۔
■ On last Friday, we traveled along with my wife, friend	■ Al-jumah-tulmaazi-nahnu-ruhna-ana-wahurmatee-	١٨ الجمعة الماضية نحن روحنا انا وحرمتي ورفيقى

English	Transliteration	Arabic
and family.	*warafeeqi-wa-aailah.*	وعائلته۔
To the sea we played and swam.	*Sobal-bahr-laibna-wa-sabahna.*	١٩ صوب البحر لعبنا وسبحنا
After that, we went to the party to eat and enjoy.	*Wabaadain-ruhna-alnaadi-li-ajli-nakulu-wanastanis.*	٢٠ وبعدين روحنا النادى لاجل ناكل ونستأنس۔
We ate fish.	*Akalna-alsamak.*	٢١ أكلنا السمك۔
After eating, my friend paid the money and we went to the cinema hall on my expense.	*Rafeeqi-dafa-alfulus-aqab-alakal-ruhna-assenima-ala-hisaab-ana.*	٢٢ رفيقى دفع الفلوس عقب الأكل روحنا السينما على حسابى أنا۔
There was an Arabic film in it.	*Kaana-feehi-film-arbi.*	٢٣ كان فيه فلم عربى۔
I couldn't watch Arabic film for a long time.	*Ana-min-zaman-ma-shuft-film - Arabi*	٢٤ أنا من زمان ما شفت فلم عربى۔
May be you watch the Arabic films?	*Yumkin-anta-shufta-aflam-arbi?*	٢٥ يمكن انت شفت أفلام عربى ؟
The film is very good.	*Alflim-kana-zain.*	٢٦ الفلم كا ن زين۔
The family took so much interest with the film.	*Aliyaal-istanaso-wajid-minal-film.*	٢٧ العيال إستانسوا واجد من الفلم۔
After watching film we were so tired.	*Aqab-alsenima-kuna-tabaneen-wajid.*	٢٨ عقب السينما كنا تعبا نين واجد۔
We went to home & slept.	*Serna-albait-wa-nimna.*	٢٩ سرنا البيت ونمنا۔
Because we were so tired.	*Li-anna-kuna-taba-nin-wajid.*	٣٠ لأن كنا تعبانين واجد۔

التدريب – I

Answer the Following questions?

1	Kam-Sana-Darasta-Al-Injiliziyah?	١ كم سنة درست الإنجليزية؟
2	Aaina-Haslata-Wazifah-Muallim?	٢ أين حصلت وظيفة معلم؟
3	Hal-Shufta-Film-Arabi?	٣ هل شفت فلم عربى؟
4	Kam-Alashya-Mujud-Fil-Bait?	٤ كم الأشياموجودة فى البيت؟

التدريب – II

Match the Following Words From Arabic to English

S.No	Roman	Arabic	English
1	Wazifah	وظيفة	Friend
2	Al-Mataar	المطار	Tickets
3	Saman	ثمن	Job
4	At-Tazakir	التذاكر	Cost
5	Rafeeq	رفيق	Airport

التدريب – III

Translate the Following Words in Arabic

S.No	English	Arabic
1	Fish	....
2	Fridge	....
3	Washing machine	....
4	Bed sheets	....
5	Arabic films	....

التدريب – IV

Translate the Following Words in English

English	Arabic	Roman	S.No
....	الشهادة	As-Shahadah	1
....	وظيفة	Wazifah	2
....	ضريبة	Dharibah	3
....	السينما	As-Cenima	4
....	نمنا	Nimna	5

Lesson-20
At The Airport

ENGLISH	ROMAN	ARABIC	S.No
Please! (Give me) ticket & passport!	*Attazkirah,waljawaz-min-fazlik!*	التذكره ، والجواز من فضلك!	١
Yes please.	*Tafazzal.*	تفضل۔	٢
Do you have Lebanon's Visa?	*Indaka-feezah-haq-Labnan.*	عندك فيزة حق لبنان۔	٣
No, I don't have.	*Laa-ma-indi.*	لا، ماعندى۔	٤
take it at the airport of the Beirut.	*Bakhozuhaa-fi-mataar-bairoot.*	باخذها فى مطار بيروت۔	٥
How many bags do you have?	*Kam-shunta-indak?*	كم شنطة عندك؟	٦
Two bags.	*Shuntatain.*	شنطتين۔	٧

English	Transliteration	Arabic
Weight this bag at the scale. 'Oh' hamid!	*Hat-hazain-shanatain-alalmeezan-ya-hamed.*	٨ حط هذين شنطين على الميزان ياحامد۔
Do you have another bag?	*Indak-shunat-saniah?*	٩ عندك شنط ثانية؟
No, I don't.	*Laa-mafi!*	١٠ لا مافى!
You have extra five kg!	*Indaka-ziyadah-Khams-kilo.*	١١ عندك زياده خمس كيلو۔
Pay 12 Dinar extra and one Dinar for airport tax.	*Idfa-esna-ashara-dinar-haqi-ziyadah-wa-dinar-wahid-zaribah-haqee-almatar.*	١٢ إدفع اثنا عشر دينار حق زيادة ودينار واحد ضريبة حق المطار۔
It's compulsory on every passenger to pay one dinar.	*Kullu-musaafir-lazim-yadfa-deenar.*	١٣ كل مسافر لازم يدفع دينار۔
Take it, these are 11 Dinar.	*Tafazzal-haza-ihdaa-ashra-deenar.*	١٤ تفضل، هذا إحدى عشر دينار۔
Fill this card then you must visit the passport department.	*Imla-e- hazihil -bataqah-wabaadainlazim-btarooh-liljawazaat.*	١٥ إملئ هذه البطاقة وبعدين لازم بتروح للجوازات۔
'O' hamid takes the bag out.	*Shail-shanat-ya-Hamid.*	١٦ شيل الشنط يا حامد۔

التدريب – I

Answer the Following questions?

1	Hal-at-tazkirah-moujoodah-indak?	هل التذكرة موجودة عندك؟	١
2	Kam-shanatah-indak?	كم شنطة عندك؟	٢
3	Hal-indak-fiza?	هل عندك فيزة؟	٣
4	Kam-dinar-lazim-likulli-musafir?	كم دينار لازم لكل مسافر؟	٤

التدريب – II

Match the Following Words From Arabic to English

S.No	Roman	Arabic	English
1	Al-Mizaan	الميزان	Dinar
2	Fiza	فيزة	Card
3	At-Tazkirah	التذكرة	Visa
4	Dinar	دينار	Ticket
5	Al-Bitaqah	البطاقة	Scale

التدريب – III

Translate the Following Words in Arabic

S.No	English	Arabic
1	Passanger	....
2	Passport department	....
3	Bag	....
4	Airport	....
5	Five kg	....

التدريب – IV

Translate the Following Words in English

English	Arabic	Roman	S.No
....	التذكرة	At-Tazkirah	1
....	الجواز	Al-Jawaz	2
....	فيزة	Fiza	3
....	مطار	Mataar	4
....	شنطة	Shantah	5

Lesson-21
World Tour

ENGLISH	ROMAN	ARABIC	S.No
Where are you travelling 'O'Hamad?	*Wain-Musafir-ya-Hamad*	وين مسافر يا حمد!	١
London! Insha'Allah.	*London-Insha'Allah*	لندن ،إنشاءالله ـ	٢
By which flight?	*Ala-ayyi-tairan?*	على أي طيران ؟	٣
Gulf air lines and you.	*Tairan-ulkhaleej- wa-anta?*	طيران الخليج وأنت ـ	٤
And I'm going to Cairo.	*Ana- ra-e-hil qahirah*	أنا رايح القاهرة ـ	٥
To which company,	*Ma'a- ayyi- sharikah?*	مع أي شركة ـ	٦
Sharaq-al-awsat.	*Sharikah-sharqul-ausat*	شركة شرق الأوسط ـ	٧
You are going directly to London?	*Anta-rahi-mubashirahtn-ila- Landon ?*	أنت راح مباشرة إلى لندن ـ	٨

English	Transliteration	Arabic
No, via Bahrain.	*La-an-tareeq-Bahrain*	٩ لا عن طريق بحرين ـ
Today night we have to stay in gulf hotel by the company.	*Binami-lailah- fi- otalil- khalij- ala- hisabi-sh sharikah*	١٠ بنام ليلة فى اوتيل الخليج على حساب الشركة ـ
Do you know anyone in London?	*Ta-aa-rif- ahad-fi-London?*	١١ تعرف أحد فى الندن ـ
Yes, I do have many friends there .	*Ayyi-na-am indi-asdeeqa- wajid- hunak.*	١٢ أي نعم عندى أصدقاء واجدهناك.
I don't know anyone in Cairo; this is the first time when I'm going to Cairo.	*Ana-ma-arif-ahad-fil- qahirah, hazihi-awwalu- marah-aruh-alqahirah .*	١٣ أنا ما أعرف أحد فى القاهرة،هذه أول مرةأروح القاهرة ـ
I advise you when you reach there say to taxi driver.	*Aqul, anta-la-taussala- honak-qul-haq-ra-e-taxi .*	١٤ أقول، أنت لتوصل هناك قول حق راعى التاكيسى ـ
To take you at hotel Haltom and. he shows you the city also.	*Yakhuzuka-ila-hotelil hiltam-wahom- yarunakal balad .*	١٥ ياخذك إلى اوتيل الهلتم وهم يرونك البلد ـ

التدريب – I

Answer the Following questions?

1	Aa'la-Ayyi-Tairan-Safara-Mohammed?	١ على أي طيران سافر محمد؟
2	Man-Yaruh-Al-Qahirah?	٢ من يروح القاهرة؟
3	Man-Yaruh-Ila-Landan?	٣ من يروح إلى لندن؟
4	Fi-Ayyi-Otail-Taskun-Al-Youm?	٤ فى أى أوتيل تسكن اليوم؟

التدريب – II

Match the Following Words From Arabic to English

S.No	Roman	Arabic	English
1	Tairan	طيران	City
2	Sharikah	شركة	Flight
3	Mubaashirah	مباشرة	Company
4	Asdiqah	أصدقاء	Direct
5	Albalad	البلد	Friends

التدريب – III

Translate the Following Words in Arabic

S.No	English	Arabic
1	Hotel	....
2	Taxi	....
3	Driver	....
4	Gulf	....
5	Today night	....

التدريب – IV

Translate the Following Words in English

English	Arabic	Roman	S.No
....	طيران	Tairaan	1
....	طيران الخليج	Tairaan Al-Khaleej	2
....	مباشرة	Mubashirah	3
....	طريق بحرين	Tariq Bahrin	4
....	راعى التاكيسى	Raea Taksi	5

Lesson-22
House

ENGLISH	ROMAN	ARABIC	S.No
I am living in a big house	*Askun-fi-bait-kabeer.*	‫أسكن فى بيت كبير‪-‬‬	١
The house is at the khaleej road Abu Dhabi	*Albeit-fi- shari- al qaleej fi- abu-zahbi.*	‫البيت فى شارع الخليج فى أبو ظبى‪-‬‬	٢
There are 5 rooms in it	*Feehi-khams-hujar.*	‫فيه خمس حجر‪-‬‬	٣
There are 3 bed rooms, 1 meeting room and 1 dining room	*Salasa-hujar-haq-num- wa-majlis-wa-hujrah- lilakl.*	‫ثلاث حجر حق نوم ‪،‬ومجلس وحجرة للأكل‪-‬‬	٤
Among the bed room one is for me &my wife	*Hujrah-min-hujr-naum- haqi-wa-haq-hurmati.*	‫حجرة من حجر النوم حقى وحق حرمتى‪-‬‬	٥
Because I'm married, I have two sons & one daughter.	*li-annani-mutazaviju-wa- indi-waladain-wa-bint.*	‫لأنى متزوج وعندى ولدين وبنت‪-‬‬	٦
The second room is for my children and another one is for my parents.	*Alhujrauts-saniah-haqi - alaolad-was-salisa-haqi- ummi- wa-abi.*	‫الحجرة الثانية حق الأولاد‪،‬الثالثة حق أمى وأبوي‪-‬‬	٧
Because they stay with us.	*Liannahum-yaskonuna-*	‫لأنهم يسكنون معنا‪-‬‬	٨

ma'ana

٩	أبوى رجال كبير عمره ستين سنة۔	• My father is old enough his age is 60 years.
		• *Abvi-rijal- kabeer- umruh-sittin- sanah.*
١٠	وأمى مرة كبيرة بعد، عمرها خمس وخمسين سنة۔	• And my mother is old enough her age is 55 years.
		• *Wa-ummi-maratun- kabirah-baad, umruha- khams- wa-khamseena- sanah.*
١١	حجرة الأكل فيها طاولة طعام وستة كراسى۔	• Dining room consists of Dining table & six chairs.
		• *Hujratul akli- fiha- tawilah- ta'am- wa- sit tah- karasi.*
١٢	المطبخ فيه الثلاجة والغسالة والفرن۔	• In the kitchen there is a fridge, washing machine, and an oven.
		• *Al-mat-bakh-fihis sallajah- wal gassalah- wal faran.*
١٣	والمجلس فيها كنبتين واربعة كراسى۔	• And in hall there are 2 sofa set and 4 chairs.
		• *Wal majlis- fiha- kanab tain- wa- arb'ah- kara si.*
١٤	حجرة النوم فيها خمس كرافيات۔	• There are 5 bed sheets in the bed room.
		• *Hujratun-nom-fiha- khams-karafiath.*
١٥	فى حمامين فى البيت، واحد كبير حقنا، والثانى الصغير حق العيال۔	• There are two bath rooms in the house, big one is for us and second small one is for my family.
		• *Fi- hamamain-filbait- wahid kabir haqna, was- sanis sager- haqqil- ayal.*

التدريب – I

Answer the Following questions?

1	Kam-Hujar-Fil-Baith?	١ كم حجر فى البيت؟
2	Liman-Al-Hujarah-As-Saniyah?	٢ لمن الحجرة الثانية؟
3	Ma-Assiyah-Al-Maujudah Fil-Almatbaq?	٣ ماالأشياء الموجودة فى المطبخ؟
4	Kam-Karafayath-Fi-Hujar-Naum?	٤ كم كرافيات فى حجرة النوم؟

التدريب – II

Match the Following Words From Arabic to English

S.No	Roman	Arabic	English
1	Al-Matbaq	المطبخ	Hall
2	Hujar	حجرة	Kitchen
3	Kanbat	كنبة	Room
4	Mutazavvij	متزوج	Sofa
5	Al-Majlis	المجلس	Married

التدريب – III

Translate the Following Words in Arabic

S.No	English	Arabic
1	Dining table	....
2	Six chairs	....
3	5 Bed sheets	....
4	Washing machine	....
5	Oven	....

التدريب – IV

Translate the Following Words in English

English	Arabic	Roman	S.No
....	رجال كبير	Rijal Kabeer	1
....	مرة كبيرة	Marrah-Kabeera	2
....	الفرن	Al-Furun	3
....	كنبتين	Kanbatain	4
....	الصغير	As-Sagheer	5

Lesson-23
At The Restaurant

ENGLISH	ROMAN	ARABIC	S.No
In the Beirut restaurant.	*Fi-matam-bairut*	فى مطعم بيروت۔	١
Welcome, please have a seat.	*Ahlan-wasahlan-tafazzalu*	أهلا وسهلاً تفضلوا۔	٢
What would you like to eat? 'O' Mubarak.	*Aish-tabi-takul-ya-mubarak*	ايش تبى تاكل؟ يامبارك۔	٣
What do you have?	*Waish fi-indikum?*	ويش فى عندكم ؟	٤
We have everything chicken, mutton, kabbab,kuba and fried fish.	*Indana-kulshai-dajaj-wa-lahm-ganam-wa kabaab-wakubba-wasmak-mashveh*	عندنا كل شيء،دجاج و لحم غنم وكباب،كُبّا والسمك مشوى۔	٥
Give me fish.	*Aatini-samk*	أعطنى السمك۔	٦
Yes, Insha'Allah.	*Hazir-Insha'Allah*	حاضر انشاءالله ۔	٧
I would like to have kabbab.	*Ana-abi-kabaab*	انا أبى كباب ۔	٨

English	Transliteration	Arabic	
Please have the salt & spice well .	*Jaib-suhun-hams-wa-suhun-saltata-min-fazlik*	جيب صحن حمص وصحن سلطة من فضلك۔	٩
Insha'Allah.	*Insha'Allah*	انشاءالله۔	١٠
What do you like to have in drink?	*Shu-tureedun-tashraboon*	شو تريدون تشربون ؟	١١
I would like to have some cool drink.	*Ana-ureed-ashrab-barid*	انا أريد أشرب با رد۔	١٢
(I think) Pepsi will be ok.	*Bepsi-zain*	بيبسى زين۔	١٣
Bring coffee after the food.	*Aatini-qahva-bada-akul*	أعطنى قهوه بعد الآكل۔	١٤
Come here 'O' boy.	*Ta-aal-ya-walad*	تعال يا ولد۔	١٥
What's the bill?	*Km-al-hisaab*	كم الحساب ؟	١٦
200 dirham.	*Miatain-dirham ?*	مائتين درهم ۔	١٧
No by Allah, I will pay the bill!	*La-wallah-anta-matadfa-ala-ana*	لا والله أنت ما تد فع على أنا!	١٨

التدريب – I

Answer the Following questions?

1	Waish-Maujood-Fi-Matam-Bairoot?	١ ويش موجود فى مطعم بيروت؟
2	Hal-Tabi-Tashrab-Barid?	٢ هل تبى تشرب بارد؟
3	Kam-Al-hisab?	٣ كم الحساب؟
4	Aish-Tabi-Takul?	٤ إيش تبى تأكل؟

التدريب – II

Match the Following Words From Arabic to English

S.No	Roman	Arabic	English
1	As-Samak	السمك	Bill
2	Kabab	كباب	Fish
3	Barid	بارد	Cold
4	Qahwah	قهوة	Kabab
5	Al-Hisab	الحساب	Coffee

التدريب – III

Translate the Following Words in Arabic

S.No	English	Arabic
1	Chicken	....
2	Mutton	....
3	Kuba	....
4	Fried fish	....
5	Spice	....

التدريب – IV

Translate the Following Words in English

English	Arabic	Roman	S.No
....	دجاج	Dajaj	1
....	لحم غنم	Lahm Ganam	2
....	السمك مشوية	As-Samk Masviya	3
....	سلطة	Saltah	4
....	كم الحساب	Kam Al-Hissab	5

Lesson-24
Over The Phone

ENGLISH	ROMAN	ARABIC	S.No
Hello, hello	*Alu-Alu*	ألوة، ألوة ـ	١
The line is not clear today.	*Alu-Alu- Alkhat-mubzain-alyom.*	الوة الوة الخط ماهو بزين اليوم ـ	٢
Who is speaking?	*Man-ya-takallam?*	من يتكلم؟	٣
I'm mohammed jasim.	*Ana-Mohammed-jasim.*	أنا محمد جاسم ـ	٤
Is this Abdullah Kaddas's house?	*Haza-bait-abdullah-kadas?*	هذا بيت عبدالله كدّاس ؟	٥
Oh yes.	*Ayyi-na-am.*	أى نعم ـ	٦
Whom you want?	*Man-tureed?*	من تريد؟	٧
I want to speak to Abdullah.	*Ureed-ahkee-abdullah*	أريد أحكى مع عبدالله ـ	٨
Ok please wait for a while.	*Zain,Esbir-suyah*	زين ، إصبر شوية ـ	٩

English	Transliteration	Arabic	
Hello.	*Alu!*	ألوة!	١٠
Welcome O Mohammed.	*Marhaban-ya-mohammed!*	مرحباً يا محمد!	١١
How are you?	*Kaifa-anta?*	كيف انت؟	١٢
Alhamdulillah.	*Alhamdulillah*	الحمد لله ـ	١٣
I am calling you for the past two hours.	*Sara-li-uhaval-attasil-fik-min muddat-saatain.*	صار لى أحاول أتصل فيك من مدة ساعتين ـ	١٤
The line was busy.	*.Walqat-mashgul*	والخط مشغول ـ	١٥
I say.	*Aqul.*	أقول ـ	١٦
Tomorrow is Friday.	*Bakir-al-jumah*	باكرالجمعة ـ	١٧
Please come with family will have fun with children & they'll enjoy.	*Tafazal, sobina-nsuloof, wa-nalab-wa-nastanis*	تفضل، صوبنا نسولف ونلعب ونستانس ـ	١٨
Ok, at what time.	*Zain-ayyi-haz?*	زين أى حظ؟	١٩
Around 9:30 clock at night.	*Hol-assa-ah tisah-wa-nisf -fil-lail.*	حولى الساعة تسعة ونصف فى الليل ـ	٢٠
Ok, fine thank you 'O' Mohammed!	*Zain-mashkur-ya mohammed.*	زين مشكور يا محمد ـ	٢١

التدريب – I

Answer the Following questions?

1	Hal-Al-Kahat-Zain-Al-Youm?	١ هل الخط زين اليوم؟
2	Mon-Yatakallam-Alal-Hatif?	٢ من يتكلم على الهاتف؟
3	Hal-Mumkin-Li-Aan-Atakalam-Min-Abdullah?	٣ هل ممكن لى أن اتكلم مع عبدالله؟
4	Mn-Yureed-Yahaki-Maa'-Abdullah?	٤ من يريد يحكى مع عبدالله؟

التدريب – II

Match the Following Words From Arabic to English

S.No	Roman	Arabic	English
1	Al-hatif	الهاتف	Hello
2	Nastanis	نستانس	Phone
3	Baith	بيت	Wait
4	Isbir	إصبر	House
5	Alu	ألوة	Enjoy

التدريب – III

Translate the Following Words in Arabic

S.No	English	Arabic
1	Line	....
2	Clear	....
3	Busy	....
4	Fun	....
5	Enjoy	....

التدريب – IV

Translate the Following Words in English

English	Arabic	Roman	S.No
....	أحكى	Aahki	1
....	إصبر	Isbir	2
....	شوية	Shuya	3
....	أتصل	Attasil	4
....	الليل	Al-Laial	5

Lesson-25
Wrong Call

ENGLISH	ROMAN	ARABIC	S.No
Ministry of Employment	*Vizarat-al-ashgaal*	وزارت الأشغال	١
Can I speak to Mr. Abdul aziz	*bi-atakalam-ma-a-saeed-abdul aziz?*	أبي أتكلم مع سيد عبد العزيز؟	٢
Do you have another number try on another number 50533456.	*Indaka-khat-sani-jarrib-raqam-50533456.*	عندك خط ثانى جرب رقم 50533456.	٣
Thank you .	*Zain-Mashkur.*	زين مشكورـ	٤
Hello abdul aziz.	*Hello-Abdul Aziz.*	ألوة ـ عبد العزيزـ	٥
Please! Is abdul aziz is available here ?	*Al-saed-abdul aziz-mujud-min-fazlik?*	السيد عبد العزيزموجود من فضلك ـ	٦
Sorry wrong number.	*Nmberah- galat, mutasif*	النمبرة غلط متأسفـ	٧
Abdul aziz is available?	*Al-saeed-abdul aziz-*	السيدعبد العزيز موجودـ	٨

maujood?

No, sorry .	*La-wallah.*	لا والله ـ	٩
Not here	*Mush- Maujud.*	مش موجودـ	١٠
He will be back after one hour.	*Beyrja-aqba-assaah*	بيرجع عقب الساعة ـ	١١
Do You have any message?	*Tabi- tatruk- lahu- resalah?*	تبى تترك له رسالة ـ؟	١٢
Yeah……	*Ayyi*	أي ـ	١٣
I want to take, about the job with him .	*Abi-Aamal-mued- vayah*	أبي أعمل موعد وياه ـ	١٤
Ok, I will convey the message .	*Zain, khalni-ashuf*	زين، خلني اشوف ـ	١٥
Tomorrow 10 'o' ok.	*Bakir-saah-ashra- zain*	باكر،ساعة عشر زين ـ	١٦
Ok, thank you.	*Zain, mashkoor*	زين ، مشكور ـ	١٧

التدريب – I

Answer the Following questions?

١   أبى أتكلم مع سيد عبدالعزيز؟

1   Abi-Atakallam-Maa'-Syed-Abdulaziz?

٢   هل عندك رقم الثانى؟

2   Hal-Indak-Raqam-Sani?

٣   هل عندك أي الرسالة؟

3   Hal-Indak-Ayyi-Risalah?

٤   فى أي الساعةلك موعد مع عبدالعزيز؟

4   Fi-Ayyi-Saa'at-laka-Maueed-Maa'-Abdulaziz

التدريب – II

Match the Following Words From Arabic to English

S.No	Roman	Arabic	English
1	Saa'ah	الساعة	Message
2	Mauid	موعد	Number
3	Khat	خط	Appointment
4	Raqham	رقم	One hour
5	Risalah	رسالة	Line

التدريب – III

Translate the Following Words in Arabic

S.No	English	Arabic
1	Wrong number	....
2	Ministry of employment	....
3	Thank you	....
4	10 ' O ' clock	....
5	Available	....

التدريب – IV

Translate the Following Words in English

English	Arabic	Roman	S.No
....	وزارت الأشغال	Wizaratu Ashqal	1
....	خط	Khat	2
....	جرب	Jarab	3
....	متأسف	Mutassif	4
....	خلنى	Khalini	5

Lesson-26
My Self

ENGLISH	ROMAN	ARABIC	S.No
▪ I'm from Manama in Bahrain	▪ *Ana-minal-Manamah-fi-Bahrain*	أنا من المنا مة فى بحرين ـ	١
▪ I studied in Manama school	▪ *Darastu-fil-manamah-fil-madrasah*	درست فى المنا مة فى المدرسة ـ	٢
▪ Primary and secondary	▪ *Alibtadayah-was-sanwiyah*	الإبتدائية و الثا نوية ـ	٣
▪ After that I left Bahrain before four years ago.	▪ *Badain-taraktu-Bahrain-qabl-arba-sineen*	بعدين تركت البحرين قبل أربع سنين ـ	٤
▪ And I came to Doha.	▪ *Wajitu-aldohah*	وجئت الدوحة ـ	٥
▪ When I reached there.	▪ *Lama-vasaltu-hina*	لما وصلت هنا ـ	٦
▪ I stayed in a house in which there are three rooms.	▪ *Sakantu-fi-manzili-fiha-salas-hujar*	سكنت فى منزل فيها ثلاث حجر ـ	٧
▪ Because I'm married	▪ *Vali-annani-mutazavij-wa-*	ولأننى متزوج وعندى عائلة	٨

	English	Transliteration	Arabic
	and I have a big family.	*indi-aailath-kabeerah*	كبيرة۔
■	And now I am living in a house near to the ocean.	■ *Wa-alhin-ana-askun-fil-baiti-qareeb-minalbahr*	٩ والحين أنا أسكن فى البيت قريب من البحر۔
■	Daily children go to the sea they play and swim.	■ *Kulluyom-al-yruhoon-sob-albahr-wa-yalaboona-wa-yusbihoon*	١٠ كل يوم الأولاد يروحون صوب *aulaad-* البحر ويلعبون ويسبحون
■	I'm a trainer.	■ *An-mudarib*	١١ أنا مُدِّرب۔
■	In the training center.	■ *Fi-markaz-it-tarbiyah*	١٢ فى مركز التدريب۔
■	For shell company.	■ *Haqi-shirkah-shil*	١٣ حق شركة شل۔

التدريب – I

Answer the Following questions?

1 Wain-Yaruh-Awlaad-Kullu-Youm?

١ وين يروح الأولاد كل يوم؟

2 Ven-Mudarrib?

٢ وين مَدرب؟

3 Fi-Ayyi-Sharika Huva-Mudarib?

٣ فى أي شركة هو مدرب؟

4 Maza-Darasta-Fi-Madrasa-Al-Manamah?

٤ ماذا درست فى مدرسة المنامة؟

التدريب – II

Match the Following Words From Arabic to English

S.No	Roman	Arabic	English
1	Madrash	مدرسة	Company
2	Al-Aulaad	الأولاد	Doha
3	Sharikah	شركة	House
4	Al-Daouha	الدوحة	Childrens
5	Manzil	منزل	School

التدريب – III

Translate the Following Words in Arabic

S.No	English	Arabic
1	Primary	....
2	Secondary	....
3	Four Years	....
4	Center	....
5	Training	....

التدريب – IV

Translate the Following Words in English

English	Arabic	Roman	S.No
....	تركتُ	Taraktu	1
....	وصلتُ	Wasaltu	2
....	مركز التدريب	Markazut Tadreeb	3
....	يسبحون	Yasbahun	4
....	يلعبون	Yala'bun	5

Lesson-27
With Friend

ENGLISH	ROMAN	ARABIC	S.No
Yesterday night me& my friend, salim.	*Amsi-fil-lail-ana-wa-sadeeqi-saalim*	أمس فى الليل أنا وصديقى سا لم ـ	١
Went to the Aiwan' restaurant 'to take food.	*Ruhuna-ila-matam (aiwaan)liajli-nakul*	روحنا إلى مطعم ''أيوان'' لأجل ناكل ـ	٢
We were so hungry and thirsty.	*Kulluna-juaneen-va-Atshaneen-wajid.*	كلنا جوعانين وعطشانين واجد ـ	٣
The Climate was very hot.	*Altaqas-kana-har-kaseer*	الطقس كان حار كثير ـ	٤
We ate chicken soup and meat then we back to the home.	*Aakalna-Maraq-wa-lahm Wa-rajana-ilal-baith*	أكلنا مرق ولحم و رجعنا إلى البيت ـ	٥

التدريب – I

Answer the Following questions?

1	Salim-Wa-Sadiquhu-Ven-Yarohaani?	سالم وصديقه وين يروحان؟ ١
2	Fi-Ayyi-Mataam-Rah-Salim-Wa-Sadiquhu?	فى أى مطعم راح سالم وصديقه؟ ٢
3	Kaif-At-Takas Al-Yaum?	كيف الطقس اليوم؟ ٣
4	Maza-Akala-Salim-Wa-Sadiqukhu-Fi-Matam?	ماذا أكل سالم وصديقه فى مطعم؟ ٤

التدريب – II

Match the Following Words From Arabic to English

S.No	Roman	Arabic	English
1	Ams	أمس	House
2	Al-lail	الليل	Yesterday
3	Sadiq	صديق	Night
4	Mataam	مطعم	Friend
5	Baith	بيت	Hotel

التدريب – III

Translate the Following Words in Arabic

S.No	English	Arabic
1	Climate	....
2	Hot	....
3	Soup	....
4	Meat	....
5	Thirsty	....

التدريب – IV

Translate the Following Words in English

English	Arabic	Roman	S.No
....	جوعانين	Jouaa'neen	1
....	عطشانين	A'tshaneen	2
....	الطقس	At-taqas	3
....	مطعم	Matam	4
....	مرق	Marq	5

Lesson-28
Meeting With Fatima

ENGLISH	ROMAN	ARABIC	S.No
Alhamdulillah peace be upon you 'O' Asma !	Alhamdulillah assalamah-ya-Asma	الحمد الله عليك السلامة-aleka- يا أسماء-	١
May Allah bless you	Allah-yusalim-alaik	ألله يسلمك-	٢
How are you?	Kaifa-haluk?	كيف حالك ؟	٣
Fine Alhamdulillah	Tayyibah- Alhumdulillah	طيبة الحمدالله-	٤
Where were you?	Wain-kunti	وين كنتِ ؟	٥
From a while I haven't seen you , almost from the since 7 years	Min zamaan-mashiftiki- minqabli-sab-a-sineen	من زمان ما شفتك من قبل سبع سنين-	٦

May Allah blessed you, I finished my secondary education six years before	*Allah-yusallimuk- khalastu -almadrasah-tas- sanvia-qabla-sitah- sanawat*	الله يسلمک خلصت المدرسة الثانوية قبل ستة سنوات ـ	٧
After that I received scholarshipfrom government and I went to America.	*Baadain-hasaltulbasah- ala-hissab-ilhukomah-wa- rahtul- America*	وبعد ين حصلت بعثة على حساب الحكومة وروحت أمريكا ـ	٨
What did you studied there?	*Waish-taalmti-hunak?*	ويش تعلمتِ هناک؟	٩
I studied English over there.	*Talam-alinjleeziah- attrbiya*	تعلم الإنجليزية التربية ـ	١٠
After receiving the certificate I came to Bahrain and I studied at teachers house for two years-	*Bada-mahasaltu- sahadah-Rajatu-al- bahrain-wa-darastu-fi- daril-muallimaat- mudahtu-sanatain*	بعد ما حصلت الشهادة رجعت البحرين ودرست فى دار المعلمات مدة سنتين ـ	١١
After that I came here ?	*Badain-jitu-hina?*	بعدين جيْت هنا؟	١٢
Oh yes! Here I'm from the past 2 years.	*Ayyi-naam, saar-li-hunak- taqreeban-sanateen*	أي نعم، صار لى هناک تقريبا سنتين ـ	١٣
Now where are you working?	*Wain-tasguleen-alheen*	وين تشغلين الحين ؟	١٤
Now I'm working in the English broadcasting department.	*Allhainll-bishtagil-fil- izaa-fi-qism-alingleeziah*	الحين بشتغل فى الإذاعة فى قسم الإنكليزية ـ	١٥

التدريب – I

Answer the Following questions?

1	Ven-kunti-min salasi-sanavath?	وين كنتِ من ثلاث سنوات؟ ١
2	Waish-ta-allamti-fil-madrasah?	ويش تعلمت فى المدرسة؟ ٢
3	Waih-tashgul-alheen?	وين تشغل الحين؟ ٣
4	Mata-Rajati-min-amrica?	متى رجعت من أمريكة؟ ٤

التدريب – II

Match the Following Words From Arabic to English

S.No	Roman	Arabic	English
1	Al-Madrasah	المدرسة	Secondary
2	As-Sanviyah	الثانوية	School
3	As-Shahadah	الشهادة	English
4	Al-Inkliziyah	الإنكليزية	Department
5	Qism	قسم	Certificate

التدريب – III

Translate the Following Words in Arabic

S.No	English	Arabic
1	School	....
2	Department	....
3	Center	....
4	Married	....
5	Message	....

التدريب – IV

Translate the Following Words in English

English	Arabic	Roman	S.No
....	خلصت	Khallastu	1
....	المدرسة	Al-Madrasah	2
....	سنوات	Sanawat	3
....	بعثة	Bao'sah	4
....	الإذاعة	Al-Eza'ah	5

Lesson-29
About Friend

ENGLISH	ROMAN	ARABIC	S.No
I have a friend his name is Saleh, he belongs to Al-Riyadh in saudia	*Indi-sadeeq-ismuh-saleh, minal-Reyadh-fi-saudiyah*	عندى صديق اسمه صالح،من الرياض فى السعودية ـ	١
My friend Saleh is married he has three children.	*Sadekhee-saleh-mutazavij-wa-indahu-salasah-ayaal*	صديقى صالح متزوج وعنده ثلاثة عيال ـ	٢
One son and two daughters	*Walad-vaahid-wabintain*	ولد واحد و بنتين ـ	٣
Saleh is 32 years old, but his wife Sheikha is 20 years only.	*Saleh-umruhu-isnain-wa-salasina-sanah-walakin-zojah-shakhia-umruhaa-ishrain sanah-bus*	صالح عمره اثنين وثلاثين سنة و لكن زوجته شيخية عمرها عشرين سنة بس ـ	٤
What is the occupation of Sheikha?	*Shiakha-ma-endha-shugul*	شيخة ماعندها شغل؟	٥
She is a housewife.	*Hia-fil-bait*	هى ربّة البيت ـ	٦

٧	• Saleh works in English company.	• *Saleh-yashtagil-ammil-fi-sharikatil-injleeziah* صالح يشتغل عامل فى شركة الإنجليزية ـ
٨	• He earns only five hundred Dirham in one month	• *Yahsolo- khamsata- miata- dirham- fish-shahri- bas* يحصل خمسة مائة درهم فى الشهر بس ـ
٩	• The father of Saleh and his mother both live with his wife and children.	• *Wa-bu-saalih-wa-ummuhu-yaskuna-ma-a-saalih-wazojah-wa-aa-ilah* أبو صالح وأمه يسكنون مع صالح وزوجتة وعائله ـ
١٠	• The house is not very big.	• *Albeit-mahuva-kabeer-wajid* البيت ماهو كبير واجد ـ
١١	• There are three bedrooms only.	• *Fihi-salaas-hujrun-naum-bus* فيه ثلاث حجر النوم بس ـ
١٢	• First one room is for Saleh and his wife, second one is for children and third one is for parents	• *Hujrah- vahda- haqi - salih-wa-hurmatihi-wa-ssani-haqi- ayaal-wa-saalis-haqi-abee-saleh-wa-ummihi* حجرة واحدة حق صالح وحرمته والثانية حق العيال وا لثالثة حق أبى صالح وأمه ـ
١٣	• There is no hall & no dining room in the house.	• *Mafi-majlis-walaa-hujratul-taaem -filbait* ما فى مجلس ولا حجرة الطعام فى البيت ـ
١٤	• There is Only one bath room.	• *Fihi-hamam-vahid-bus* فيه حمام واحد بس ـ

التدريب – I

Answer the Following questions?

1	Kam-Umaru-Saleh?		كم عمر صالح؟ ١
2	Hal-Li-Shekha-Ayyi-Amal?		هل لشيخة أي عمل؟ ٢
3	Fi-Ayyi-Sharikah-yamal-Saleh?		في أي شركة يعمل صالح؟ ٣
4	Kam-Dirham-Yahslu-Saleh-Fis-Shahr?		كم درهم يحصل صالح في الشهر؟ ٤

التدريب – II

Match the Following Words From Arabic to English

S.No	Roman	Arabic	English
1	Al-bait	البيت	Mother
2	Hujar	حجر	House
3	Ayyal	عيال	Rooms
4	Hurmah	حرمة	Relatives
5	Umm	أَمَ	Wife

التدريب – III

Translate the Following Words in Arabic

S.No	English	Arabic
1	Hall	....
2	Dining room	....
3	Bath room	....
4	House wife	....
5	Married	....

التدريب – IV

Translate the Following Words in English

English	Arabic	Roman	S.No
....	عيال	A'yaal	1
....	عامل	Aa'mil	2
....	شركة	Sharikah	3
....	الإنجليزية	Al-Injiliziyah	4
....	يسكنون	Yaskunoon	5

Lesson-30
For Leave

ENGLISH	ROMAN	ARABIC	S.No
How are you Saleh?	*Waish-fik-ya-saleh?*	ويش فيك يا صالح ؟	١
Are you Sick?	*Aanta- Mareez?*	أنت مريض؟	٢
No, I am not sick but I am tired.	*La,ma-Ana,bi-maReez-tabaan-wajid*	لا، ماانا بمريض تعبان واجد ـ	٣
Take leave and go to Beirut or Cairo and London or Tunis.	*Khuz-rukhsah-wasaafir-ila-bairut-awo alkhahirah-wa-london-wa-rooh-tonis*	خذ رخصة وسا فر إلى بيروت أوالقا هرة ولالندن أو روح تونس ـ ـ	٤
Ok, May Allah have peace upon you.	*Adl-Allah-yusallimuk*	عدل ألله يسلمك ـ	٥
I applied to take the leave.	*Ana-Qadamtu-talab- haq-alijazah*	أنا قدمَّت طلب حق الإجازةـ	٦
But, it's necessary that the manager should	*Almudeer-lazim-yuwafiq*	المدير لازم يوافق ـ	٧

agree.

- I am saying, the manager is very good person, he likes and helps every one.
- *Aqul- almudeer-qwesh-rijal, yuhibbu-wa-usayaaid-kul-wahid*

٨ أقُول ،المدير خوش رجال ،يحب ويساعد كل واحد۔

- He also helped me last year.
- *Saadani-alaam almazi*

٩ ساعدنى العام الماضى۔

- I got leave, last year.
- *Hasaltu-alijazah,fi- al-aam- almaazi*

١٠ حلصت الإجازة، فى العام الماضى۔

- I am sure, that my opinion would be the same .
- *Aana-mutakid-ana- raaie -muwafq*

١١ أنا متأكد أنا رائى موافق۔

- Where do you want to travel?
- *Wain-raih-tusaafir?*

١٢ وين رايح تسافر؟

- Cairo insha-Allah.
- *Al-khahirah- Insha'Allah*

١٣ القاهرة إنشاءالله ۔

- On Friday.
- *Ma-aljumah*

١٤ مع الجمعة ۔

- No, today is good.
- *La-biroohi-Alyaom-ahsan*

١٥ لا، بروحى اليوم أحسن۔

- I went to Cairo in last summer.
- *Ana-safartu-alQhahi-rah- alsaif-al-mazee-ba-ad*

١٦ أنا سافرت القاهرة الصيف الماضى بعد۔

التدريب – I

Answer the Following questions?

1	Ma-Hanat-Li-Saleh?	١	ما حانت لصالح؟
2	Aena-Tusafir?	٢	أين تسافر؟
3	Mata-Hasala-Al-Ijazah-Sadeeq-Saleh?	٣	متى حصل الإجازة صديق صالح؟
4	Aena-Safar-Saleh-Fis-Saif-Al-Mazi?	٤	أين سافر صالح في الصيف الماضى؟

التدريب – II

Match the Following Words From Arabic to English

S.No	Roman	Arabic	English
1	Tunis	تونس	Good
2	Mariz	مريض	Tunis
3	Al-Shurti	الشرطي	Sick
4	Muwafiq	موافق	Manager
5	Ahsan	أحسن	Same

التدريب – III

Translate the Following Words in Arabic

S.No	English	Arabic
1	Summer	....
2	Leave	....
3	Opinion	....
4	Last year	....
5	Necessary	....

التدريب – IV

Translate the Following Words in English

English	Arabic	Roman	S.No
....	مريض	Mariz	1
....	تعبان	Taa'baan	2
....	سافر	Safir	3
....	المحاسب	Al-Muhasab	4
....	متأكد	Mutaakkid	5

Lesson-31
Post Office

ENGLISH	ROMAN	ARABIC	S.No
Peace be upon you	*Assalamualekum*	السلام عليكم۔	١
Same to you	*Walekum-assalam*	وعليكم السلام۔	٢
Can I ask you a question?	*Mum-kin-as-aluka-suaal?*	ممكن أسئلك سوال؟	٣
Yes Please.	*Tafazzal*	تفضل!	٤
Can you tell me that where is Post office?	*Mumkin-taquli-wain-maktab-ul-bareed*	ممكن تقول لى وين مكتب البريد؟	٥
How would you like to go? By walk or car.	*Anta-Tabi- tamshi-wala-tabit- tarooh- bis-sayyarah?*	أنت تبى تمشى ولا تبى تروح باالسيارة؟	٦
I would like to go by car.	*Ab-Aruh-bis-sayyarah*	أبى أروح بالسيارة۔	٧
O.k.	*Zain*	زين۔	٨

English	Transliteration	Arabic	
This is shaik zaid road.	*Hazihi-shari-zaid?*	هذه شارع زائد ـ	٩
Take reverse from here.	*Reayos- huna*	ريوس هنا ـ	١٠
After that, go straight.	*Wa-baadain-rooh-alaa-tool*	وبعدين روح على طول ـ	١١
There is x road.	*Li-tusil-Al-jalah*	لتوصل الجولة ـ	١٢
After that.	*Wa-badain*	وبعدين ـ	١٣
Turn to the north.	*Leef-Ala-shamal*	لف على الشمال ـ	١٤
Walk some, you would find two buildings.	*Imshi-shoya-yatahsal-bina-yateen*	إمشى شوى يتحصل بنايتين ـ	١٥
The right side building is American Embassy.	*ala-yumink, alsifarah-ilal-Americiyah*	على يمينك السفارة الأمريكية ـ	١٦
And your left side there is one building.	*Qalha,va-daish-albinayah-Li-Ala-shimalik*	خلها، ودش البناية لعلى شمالك ـ	١٧
In that building the Post Office is at second floor.	*Maktab-al-bareed-fi-ttabiq-alsani*	مكتب البريد فى الطابق الثانى ـ	١٨
Thank you.	*Mashkoor*	مشكور ـ	١٩
Allah is with you.	*Allah -wayaak*	الله وياك ـ	٢٠

التدريب – ١

Answer the Following questions?

1	Haal-Laka-Ayyi-Aamal-Fi-maktabul-barid?	هل لك أي عمل فى مكتب البريد؟ ١
2	Anta-tabi-tamshi-wala-tabi-taruh-bisiyyarah?	أنت تبى تمشى ولاتبى تروح بالسيارة؟ ٢
3	Fi-Ayyi-Tabiq-Maktab-Ul-Bareed Maujud?	فى أي الطابق مكتب البريد موجود ؟ ٣
4	Ven-Maktab-Ul-Bareed?	أين مكتب البريد؟ ٤

التدريب – II

Match the Following Words From Arabic to English

S.No	Roman	Arabic	English
1	As-sayyarah	السيارة	Embassy
2	As-suwal	السوال	Car
3	As-sani	الثانى	Question
4	At-tabiq	الطابق	Second
5	As-safarah	السفارة	Floor

التدريب – III

Translate the Following Words in Arabic

S.No	English	Arabic
1	Second floor	....
2	Post office	....
3	Building	....
4	X Road	....
5	Road	....

التدريب – IV

Translate the Following Words in English

English	Arabic	Roman	S.No
....	يسئلك	Yas-Aluka	1
....	أمشى	Aamshi	2
....	ريوس	Reuoos	3
....	يتحصل	Yatahassal	4
....	المنزل	Al-manzil	5

Lesson-32
The American Embassy

ENGLISH	ROMAN	ARABIC	S.No
▪ May Allah provide you with best reward (may you have long life)	▪ *Khul-li-ya taweelal-umar*	قل لى يا طويل العمر	١
▪ The American Embassy is so far from here	▪ *Alsafarah-al-Amriciyah-baeedun-min-huna*	السفارة الأمريكية بعيدة من هنا	٢
▪ Yes, I swear it so far from here	▪ *Ayyi-wallah-baeedh-wajid*	أي والله بعيدة واجد	٣
▪ If you are hurry take the taxi	▪ *Iza-antah-mustajil-khuz-taksi*	إذا أنت مستعجل خذ تاكسى	٤
▪ No, I have a car	▪ *La,indi, sayyarah*	لا،عندى،سيارة	٥
▪ And i don't no the way of Embassy	▪ *Walakin-ma-arif-Al-sifarah*	ولكن ما أعرف السفارة	٦

■ Ok ,now you are in the south of the city	■ *Zain, antafi-junoobil-madeenah*	٧ زين، أنت فى جنوب المدينة
■ The American Embassy is in northern side of the city	■ *Alsifarah-al-Amriciyah-fi-shimalil madeenah*	٨ السفارة الأمريكية فى شمال المدينة
■ It means, so far	■ *Yani-aamamak*	٩ يعنى أمامك
■ Ok,I must go straight	■ *Ayyi-lazim-arooh-ala- tuol*	١٠ أيّ لا زم أروح على طول
■ In this way	■ *Hakaza*	١١ هكذا
■ O.k.	■ *Adl*	١٢ عدل
■ Go straight almost one kilo Meter distance	■ *Ruh-ala- tuol, taqreeban-musaafah- kilo-meter*	١٣ روح على طول تقريبا مسافة كيلو ميتر
■ And after second X road, turn to the northern side	■ *Wabadain-inda jolah-alsaniya, leef-ala aeedek-alshimal*	١٤ وبعدين عند جولة الثانية لف على أيدك الشمال
■ Thank you	■ *Mashkoor*	١٥ مشكور
■ Thank you	■ *Mamnoon*	١٦ ممنون.

التدريب – I
Answer the Following questions?

1	Hal-Asafaratul-Amriciyah-Baeeda-Min-Hina?	١ هل السفارة الامريكية بعيدة من هنا؟
2	Hal-Asafaratul-amriciyah-fi-shimal-almadina	٢ هل السفارة الأمريكية فى شمال المدينة؟
3	Hal-anta-mustajil?	٣ هل انت مستعجل؟
4	Kam-masafath-lis-sifarah-al-amrica?	٤ كم مسافة للسفارة الامريكة؟

التدريب – II
Match the Following Words From Arabic to English

S.No	Roman	Arabic	English
1	Baeedah	بعيدة	North
2	Shimal	شمال	Far
3	Almadina	المدينة	Embassy
4	Masafah	مسافة	City
5	As-Sifarah	السفارة	Distance

التدريب – III
Translate the Following Words in Arabic

S.No	English	Arabic
1	Hurry	....
2	South	....
3	Almost	....
4	Distance	....
5	Carpenter	....

التدريب – IV
Translate the Following Words in English

English	Arabic	Roman	S.No
....	السفارة السعودية	As-sifarah-al-saudiya	1
....	بعيدة	Baa'eedah	2
....	ما أعرف	Ma aa'rif	3
....	أمامك	Aamaamak	4
....	كيلو ميتر	Kilo-Mitar	5

Lesson-33
Ramadhan Eid

ENGLISH	ROMAN	ARABIC	S.No
Yesterday, Abu Salim wanted to go to market	*Awal-lil-ams-abu-salim-baga-yaruhooh-alsoq*	أول الأمس أبو سالم بغى يروح السوق۔	١
The car was defective.	*Sayyarah-kanat-qarbaniah*	سيارة كانت خربانة۔	٢
He went to the market and bought meat for family.	*Masha-ila-alsuq-wa-ishtara lahm-haq -al aailahi*	مشى الى السوق واشترى لحم، حق عائلته۔	٣
And then he bought sweet dress, and shoe for his wife and child.	*Wa-bad-ishtara-halwa-wa-hadum-wa-javatee-haqi-waladah-wa-hurmatahi*	وبعد اشترى حلوى وهدوم وجواتى حق ولده و حرمتة۔	٤
Because, tomorrow is Eid-e-Ramadan	*Lianah-bakir-Eid-Ramdan*	لأنه باكر عيد رمضان۔	٥
May Allah have peace upon you, the people were well dressed what they have in Eid-e-Ramadan.	*Wannas-Allah-yusallimuk-fi-Eid-Ramzan-yalbasun-ahsan-shai-indahum*	والناس ألله يسلمك فى عيد رمضان يلبسون أحسن شئ عندهم۔	٦

■ They goes to their family, and stay with them and drink coffee.	■ *Yaruhun-wa-yashfun-Ahalahum-wa-yusaulafoon-wa-yashraboon-gahwa*	٧ يروحون ويشفون أهلهم، و يسولفون ويشربون قهوة۔
■ Abu Salim came back from market.(his wife told him)	■ *Busalim-lama raja-minaslsoq-marath-hu-qalat-lahu*	٨ أبوسالم لما رجع من السوق مرأته قالت له ۔
■ 'O' Abu Salim' you didn't bought the milk.	■ *Laish-mashtaraita-alhaleeb-ya-abu salim*	٩ ليش مااشتريت الحليب يا أبوسالم۔
■ Abu Salim said, by Allah I forgot.	■ *Busalim-qala-wa-Allah-naseet*	١٠ أبوسالم قال والله نسيت
■ once again Abu Salim wanted to go to the market.	■ *Busalim-baga-yaruh-alsoq-sani-marrah*	١١ أبوسالم بغى يروح السوق ثانى مرة۔
■ But his wife said, Let it be.	■ *Walakin-marathu-qalat-lahu*	١٢ ولكن مرأتة قالت له ۔
■ Go tomorrow. We have some milk remaining from yesterday.	■ *Taruh-bakir-indana-suuya-haleeb-baqi-min-ams*	١٣ تروح باكر عندنا شوية حليب باقى من أمس۔

التدريب – ١

Answer the Following questions?

1	Ven-Abu Salim-Baga-Yaruh?	١ وين أبوسالم بغى يروح؟
2	Hal-As-Saiyarah-Kharbanah?	٢ هل السيارة خربانة؟
3	Mata-Eid-Ramazan?	٣ متى عيد رمضان؟
4	Hal-Istari-Abu-Salim-Al-Haleeb?	٤ هل إشترى أبوسالم الحليب؟

التدريب – II

Match the Following Words From Arabic to English

S.No	Roman	Arabic	English
1	Eid	عيد	Wife
2	Haleeb	حليب	Festival
3	Sayyarah	سيارة	Milk
4	As-Suqh	السوق	Car
5	Hurmah	حرمة	Market

التدريب – III

Translate the Following Words in Arabic

S.No	English	Arabic
1	Tommorow	....
2	Sweet	....
3	Coffee	....
4	Yesterday	....
5	Dress	....

التدريب – IV

Translate the Following Words in English

English	Arabic	Roman	S.No
....	بغى	Bagha	1
....	إشترى	Eshtara	2
....	نسيت	Naseetu	3
....	لبن	Laban	4
....	باقى	Baqhii	5

Lesson-34
Festival

ENGLISH	ROMAN	ARABIC	S.No
▪ Why tomorrow is holiday O' Khamees	▪ *Laish-fi-utlah-bakir-ya kamees*	ليش في عطلة باكر يا خميس	١
▪ Tomorrow is Eid-e-Ramadan, May you have long life	▪ *Bakir-Eid-Ramdan-ya-taveel-umr*	باكر عيد رمضان يا طويل العمر	٢
▪ Ok, you have Eid festival, Welcome Eid Festival	▪ *Ayyi-Adl, Eduk-mubarak*	أيّ عدل، عيدك مبارك،	٣
▪ May you have good health every year O' William	▪ *Kullu-aam-antum-bikhair-ya wilyam*	كل عام وأنتم بخير يا وليم	٤

English	Transliteration	Arabic
You have another festival also	*fi-Aayad-sanian-endakum-hina*	في أعياد ثانية عندكم هنا ٥
May Allah have peace upon you we have another eid ul azha	*Allah-yusallimk-fi-Eid-il-azha,*	ألله يسلمك في عيدالأضحي ٦
And you are in America, how many Eid are there?	*Wa-antum-fi-america, waish-fi- aayad-indukum*	وأنتم في امريكا، ويش فى أعياد عندكم؟ ٧
We have two great festivals, Christmas and new year.	*Indana-Eidain-kabirain, Eidulmaylad, yanee-karasmas, wa-Eidrais-alsanah, yani-new year*	عندنا عيدين كبيرين، عيد الميلاد ، يعني كرسمس ، وعيد رائس السنة ، يعني نيو إير ٨
What do the people do in these festivals?	*Waish-yafalun-alnas-fi-hazihil-aayaad*	ويش يفعلون الناس في هذه الأعياد؟ ٩
May Allah have peace upon you, they go to the mosque offer Namaz and recite the Glorious Qur'an .	*Allah-yusallimuk-fi-lsabaah-yaruhun-almasjid-yousalun, wayaqraunal-Quraan*	ألله يسلمك في الصباح يروحون المسجد يصلون ، ويقرٰون القرآن ١٠
After that they go and come back,to their family and friends, they go to the park and public garden.	*Wa-badain-yaruhun-wa-yo-eeduna-ala-ahlihim-wa-asdiqihim, wa-yaruhun-al-muntazihaat-wa-hadaaiq-alaamah.*	وبعدين يروحون ويعيدون على أهلهم وأصدقائهم ، ويروحون المنتزهات والحدائق العامة ـ ١١

التدريب – I

Answer the Following questions?

1	Limaza-kanat-utlah?	١ لماذا كانت عطلة؟
2	Kam-aayad-indakum?	٢ كم أعياد عندكم؟
3	Waish-Yafaloon-Anaas-Fi -Al-Aayad?	٣ ويش يفعلون الناس فى الأعياد؟
4	Mata-Eid-Ramazan?	٤ متى عيد رمضان؟

التدريب – II

Match the Following Words From Arabic to English

S.No	Roman	Arabic	English
1	Bakir	باكر	Good
2	As-Sabah	الصباح	Tomorrow
3	Al-Quran	القرآن	Morning
4	Laham	لحم	Al-Quran
5	Aayadh	أعياد	Mutton

التدريب – III

Translate the Following Words in Arabic

S.No	English	Arabic
1	New year	....
2	Park	....
3	Public garden	....
4	Christmas	....
5	Holiday	....

التدريب – IV

Translate the Following Words in English

English	Arabic	Roman	S.No
....	الناس	An-Naas	1
....	يصلون	Yusalun	2
....	يقرؤون	Yaqraoon	3
....	المسجد	Al-Masjid	4
....	مبارك	Mubarak	5

Lesson-35
Outing

ENGLISH	ROMAN	ARABIC	S.No
Where did you go yesterday I could not see you?	*Wain- ruhata- amsi- ma- shuftuka?*	وين روحت أمس ما شفتک	١
We all went to club	*Ruhatu-ma-al- jama'ati- ilan- Nadi*	روحت مع الجماعة إلى النادى۔	٢
What did you do there?	*Waish- amiltum- hunak*	ويش عملتم هناك۔	٣
By Allah, we took fishing boat and went to the sea for fishing, after that we came back to the club.	*Wallahi- akhazna- jalbut-wa- ruhana- al bahra- wa- sadnas- samak- wa- baden- rajanan- nadi*	والله أخذنا جلبوت وروحنا البحر وصدنا السمک وبعدين رجعنا al النادى۔	٤
I informed you that there was nobody in home.	*Ana- khabartuka- fil- baiti- ma- kana- fi- ahad*	أنا خابرتک في البيت ماكان فى أحد۔	٥

التدريب – I
Answer the Following questions?

1	Ven-Roohta-Youm-Ussabt?	وين روحتَ يوم السبت؟ ١
2	Maza-Aamiltum-Fil-Utlah?	ماذا عملتم فى العطلة؟ ٢
3	Hal-Akaaztum-Jalbut?	هل اخذتم جلبوت؟ ٣
4	Hal-Fi-Baiti-Ayi-Wahid-Mujud?	هل فى البيت أي واحد موجود؟ ٤

التدريب – II
Match the Following Words From Arabic to English

S.No	Roman	Arabic	English
1	Ams	أمس	Ocean
2	Jalbut	جلبوت	Group
3	Jama'ah	جماعة	Boat
4	An-Nadi	النادى	Yesterday
5	Al-Bahr	البحر	Club

التدريب – III
Translate the Following Words in Arabic

S.No	English	Arabic
1	Holiday	....
2	Club	....
3	Wednesday	....
4	Hurry	....
5	House wife	....

التدريب – IV
Translate the Following Words in English

English	Arabic	Roman	S.No
....	الجماعة	Al-Jamaah	1
....	عملتم	A'miltum	2
....	جلبوت	Jalbut	3
....	السمک	As-Samak	4
....	الخبر	Al-Kabar	5

Lesson-36
In Post Office

ENGLISH	ROMAN	ARABIC	S.No
Where is the post office please?	*Wain- maktabul- bareed- min- fazlak*	وين مكتب البريد من فضلك؟	١
It's straight.	*Zaika-assawb.*	ذاك الصوب.	٢
I want to send this letter to England.	*Oreedu-atrish-hazal- tarad-ila-Inkltara*	أريد أطرش هذا الطرد إلى إنكلترا	٣
Do you want to send it by normal post or speed post?	*Tureedu-aadi-wala-juwai?*	تريد عادي ولاجوي؟	٤
By Speed post, please.	*Jawai-min-fazlak*	جوي من فضلك.	٥
Ok, this stamp is five dirham	*Zain-haza-tabi3-5 dirham.*	زين هذا طابع ٥ درهم.	٦
Have a seat please.	*Tafazzal*	تفضل!	٧

English	Transliteration	Arabic
I have a parcel and I want to send it to the Kuwait.	*Indi-tarred-oreed-at-resh-ila-Kuwait.*	عندى طرد أريد أطرش إلى الكويت. ٨
Go to the second window	*Ruh-nafiza-sania*	روح النافذة الثانية. ٩
I want to send this parcel to the Kuwait.	*Abi-atrash-haza-at- tarda-ill-kuwait*	أبى أطرش هذا الطرد الى الكويت. ١٠
What is in it?	*Waish-fi-dakhila*	ويش فى داخلة؟ ١١
Books and papers.	*Kutub-wa-awraq*	كتب وأوراق. ١٢
By the speed post or ship post?	*Juwai-wala-bil-bahr?*	جوى ولا بالبحر. ١٣
By normal registed ship post.	*Aadi-bil-bahr-bas-musajjal.*	عادى بالبحر بس مسجل ١٤
Ok, please weight on the scale.	*Zain-hatti-alal-meezan*	زين حط على الميزان. ١٥
This is 2 kilo and 50 gram .	*Haza-kilwain-wa-khamseen-geeram*	هذا ٢ كيلو وخمسين غرام. ١٦
It would cost ten dirham	*Yukallifu-10- dirhm- bus*	يكلف 10 درهم بس. ١٧
Ok, when it would reach?	*Tafazzal- mata- yosal?*	تفضل متى يوصل؟ ١٨
After two or three months Inshallah	*Insha allah- aqb- sherain-wala- salasah*	إنشاالله عقب شهرين ولاثلاثة. ١٩

التدريب – I

Answer the Following questions?

1	Ven-Maktabul-Barid?Wa-Mal -Masafah?	١ وين مكتب البريد؟وما المسافة؟
2	Tureed-Tursil-Aadi-Wala-Javi?	٢ تريد ترسل عادى ولاجوى؟
3	Waish-Fi-Dhakihla?	٣ ويش فى داخلة؟
4	Mata-Yusil-Hazihi-ila-Inkaltarah?	٤ متى يوصل هذه إلى إنكلترة؟

التدريب – II

Match the Following Words From Arabic to English

S.No	Roman	Arabic	English
1	Aa'di	عادى	Gram
2	Dakhilah	داخلة	Normal
3	Jawi	جوى	Inside
4	Meezaan	ميزان	Speed
5	Gharam	غرام	Scale

التدريب – III

Translate the Following Words in Arabic

S.No	English	Arabic
1	Ship post	....
2	Speed post	....
3	Normal post	....
4	Parcel	....
5	South	....

التدريب – IV

Translate the Following Words in English

English	Arabic	Roman	S.No
....	مكتب البريد	Maktabul-Bareed	1
....	أطرش	Athrash	2
....	إنكلترا	Inkaltara	3
....	النافذة الثانية	An-Nafiza-Asaniya	4
....	الميزان	Al-Mizaan	5

Lesson-37
Gulf

ENGLISH	ROMAN	ARABIC	S.No
Tell me about Gulf what is it?	*Qul-li-Aan- khalijil-arabi- waish-yani*	قول لي ، عن خليج العربى ويش يعنى؟	١
The Gulf means Arabian countries that are called Gulf.	*Alkhalijul- arabi- yani- albuldanul- arabiyyah-li- alal- khalij*	الخليج العربى يعنى البلدان العربية لعلى الخليج۔	٢
Gulf is called for ocean.	*Khalij- tadri- yani- al-bahar*	خليج تدري يعنى البحر۔	٣
How many countries are coming under it.	*Waish- hiyal- buldan- waish- fiha?*	ويش هي البلدان ويش فيها؟	٤
These are those countries, you studied about them in geography, do you want to take my test?	*Haza- waish- darsata- fil- jagrafiyyah- anta-tabi - tamtahini*	هذا ويش درست في الجغرافيا انت تبى تمتحنى؟	٥

٦	No, by Allah may you have the long life; I don't know about this my father taught me about (years ago).	*La- wallahi- tala- umruka- ana- ma- adri- abi- ta allamani*	لا والله طال عمرك أنا ماأدرى أبى تعلمنى۔
٧	Ok, then the countries are these,Qatar' Bahrain 'Oman' emirates' etc.	*Zain, albuldan' hiya'qatar-wal-bahrain- wa-oman-wal-Emarat-wa- gairiha*	زين، البلدان،هي قطرو البحرين و عمان و الإمارات، وغيرها۔
٨	Can you tell me something about Abu Dhabi?	*Mumkin- taqooli- shai-an- abi- zahbi*	ممكن تقولى شئ عن أبوظبي
٩	Yes, may Allah have peace be upon you, Abu Dhabi is the capital of emirates.	*Ayyi-nam- bu zahabi- allahu- yusallimuk- hiyal- aasimah-alemarat*	أي نعم أبوظبي الله يسلمک هي العاصمة الإمارات
١٠	Capital that's city' there is the king may Allah give him a long life, and his government also	*Al-aasimah- yan-i al- madeenah' fihal- hakim- taweelal umari' dawa-e-i- ral hukumah*	العاصمة يعنى المدينة' فيها الحاكم طويل العمر'والدوائر الحكومة
١١	Ok, now I am busy let me go next time I shall tell you about the Bahrain and Qatar may you be in the safety of Allah	*Zain- alheen- indi- shugl' Astarkhisu- waqtas- sani- oallimuk- aan-Qatar-wal- Bahrain-fi-Amanillah*	زين الحين عندى شغل' أسترخص وقت الثاني أعلمک عن قطروالبحرين في أمان الله.
١٢	God bless you, good bye	*Barakallahu- fika- ma- assalamah*	بارک الله فيک مع السلامة

التدريب – I

Answer the Following questions?

1	Waish-Albudan-Fi-Khaleej-Al-Arabi?	١ ويش البلدان فى خليج العربى؟
2	Shu-Esmu-Al'asimah?	٢ شو إسم العاصمة؟
3	Khul-Shain-An-Abudahbi?	٣ قل شأ عن أبوظبى؟
4	Hal-Indak-Shugal-Alheen?	٤ هل عندك شغل الحين؟

التدريب – II

Match the Following Words From Arabic to English

S.No	Roman	Arabic	English
1	Buldan	بلدان	Ocean
2	Al-bahr	البحر	Countries
3	A'simah	عاصمة	City
4	Madinah	مدينة	Work
5	shugal	شغل	Capital

التدريب – III

Translate the Following Words in Arabic

S.No	English	Arabic
1	Gulf	....
2	Government	....
3	Long life	....
4	Emirates	....
5	Geography	....

التدريب – IV

Translate the Following Words in English

English	Arabic	Roman	S.No
....	بارك الله	Barak Allah	1
....	والله	Wallahi	2
....	العاصمة	Al-Aasimah	3
....	يعنى	Yani	4
....	ويش	Waish	5

Lesson-38
Qatar And Bahrain

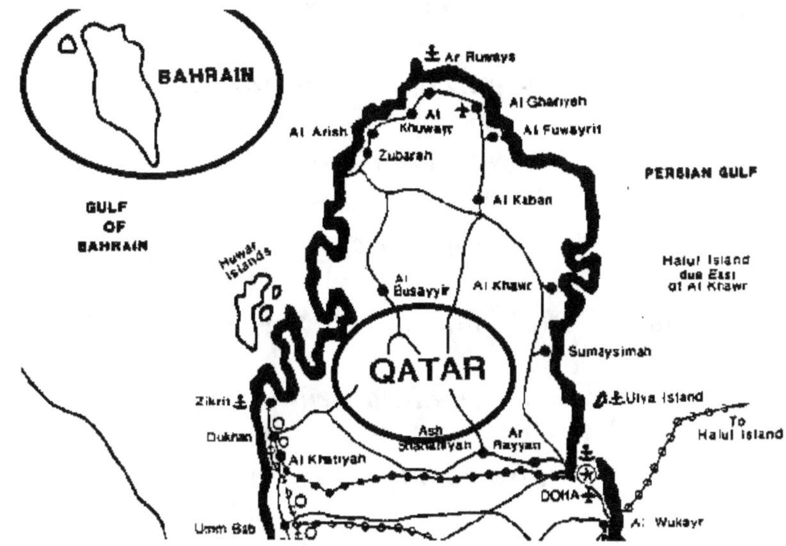

ENGLISH	ROMAN	ARABIC	S.No
Qatar and Bahrain are near from Abu Dhabi.	*Qatar- wa- Bahrain- qareebain- min- bo zahbi*	قطر وبحرين قريبين من أبو ظبى۔	١
There is half hour's distance from Abu Dhabi to Qatar by the aeroplane and half hour from Qatar to Bahrain.	*Min- bo zahbi- ila- Qatar- hawalai- nisfu- sa'ah- bit tayyarah- wa- nisfu- sa'ah- min- Qatar- lil Bahrain*	من أبو ظبى إلى قطر حوالى نصف ساعة بالطيارة ونصف ساعة من قطر للبحرين۔	٢
The capital of Qatar is Doha.	*Aasimatu- Qatar-Al- Dawha*	عاصمة قطر الدوحة۔	٣
Doha is a beautiful city there are gardens trees and beautiful scenes.	*Addawha- madeenath- jameelah- fiha- basateen- wa- shajar- wa- manazirun- hulwah*	الدوحة مدينة جميلة فيها بساتين وشجر ومناظر حلوة۔	٤

	English	Transliteration	Arabic
٥	In the zoo of Doha, there is lion, tiger, elephant, deer, monkeys and other animals.	*Hadeeqatul- haiwanat- fid- dawha- fiha- asadun- wa- namirun- wa- filun- wa- gazlanun- wa- qurud- wa- haiwanat- sania*	حديقة الحيوانات فى الدوحة فيها أسد ونمر وفيل وغزلان قرود وحيوانات ثانية ـ
٦	The weather in Doha is dry, that's from Abu Dhabi but in the Bahrain the summer is same.	*Al-hawa- fid –dawha- ajaf, min- bu zahbi wa-fil-bahrain-al-haurru-nafsus-shai*	الهواء فى الدوحة أجف، من أبوظبى وفى البحرين الحر نفس الشئي ـ
٧	Bahrain is Island not mainland.	*Albahrain- jazeerath- wala- shbah-jazeerah*	البحرين جزيرة ولاشبة جزيرة ـ
٨	May you have the long life, Bahrain is a general island.	*Albahrain- tala- umruka- jazeerat- awdah*	البحرين طال عمرك جزيرة عودة ـ
٩	In fact, there are eleven Islands in Bahrain not more and nor less, may Allah knows better.	*Fil-haqeeqath-albahrain-Ehda-ashara-jazeerah- la- aksar-awo-aqal-wallahi-ma- adri*	فى الحقيقة البحرين إحدى عشرة جزيرة لا أكثر أو أقل والله ماأدرى ـ
١٠	Manamah is the capital of Bahrain and Manama is a big Island.	*Almanamah-aasimatu-bahrain-wal-manamah akbaru-jazeerah*	المنامة عاصمة بحرين والمنامة أكبر جزيرة ـ
١١	Muharriq is smaller than Manama.	*Almuharriq-asgaru-minal-manamah*	المحرق أصغر من المنامة ـ
١٢	The atmosphere is so humid in Bahrain.	*Aljauu-fil Bahrain- rutubah-wajid.*	الجو فى البحرين فيه رطوبة واجد ـ

Now I am working in a 'bosco' company.	*Ana-alheen-Ashtagil-fi-sharikah-baskoo*	١٣ أنا الحين أشتغل فى شركة باسكو۔
Before that, I worked as a mechanic in the island of Das, and it is near to Abu Dhabi	*Qabla- kuntu- ashtagil- mekaniki- fi- jazeerati- das- wahiya- aqrab- ila- abu zahbi*	١٤ قبل كنت أشتغل ميكانكى فى جزيرة داس وهى أقرب إلى أبوظبى۔
How many kind of fishes are in the Gulf?	*Waish- anwaus- samak- fil- Al-khaleej?*	١٥ ويش أنواع السمك فى الخليج؟
May Allah have peace be upon you, everything is well about gulf's fishes.	*Samak-ul- khaleej- allahu- yusallimuk- kulla- shai- zain- tayyib.*	١٦ سمك الخليج الله يسلمك كلشي زين طيب۔
There is bity, Sabi, Hamoor, Tan'aj and Ruban, these are the name of fishes in the gulf.	*Fihi-baiti- wa- sab-i wa- hamoor- wa- tanaj- wa ruban- wa- hazihi – asmau- samak – khaleej.*	١٧ فيه بيتى، وصبى،وهامور، وتنعج،وربعان وهذه أسماء سمك الخليج۔

التدريب – I
Answer the Following questions?

1	Hal-qatar-wa-bahrain-qhareebain-min-abu-zahbi?	هل قطر وبحرين قريبين من ابوظبى؟ ١
2	Waish-Anwaa'-As-Samak-Fil-Khaleej?	ويش أنواع السمك فى الخليج؟ ٢
3	Kaif-Kanat-Al-Hawa-Fid-Doha?	كيف كانت الهواء فى الدوحة؟ ٣
4	Hal-Ad-Doha-Madina-Jameelah?	هل الدوحة مدينة جميلة؟ ٤

التدريب – II
Match the Following Words From Arabic to English

S.No	Roman	Arabic	English
1	Al-Manamah	المنامة	Dry
2	Anwaa'	أنواع	Fish
3	As-samak	السمک	Kinds
4	Akber	أكبر	Manamah
5	Aajaf	أجف	Big

التدريب – III
Translate the Following Words in Arabic

S.No	English	Arabic
1	Atmosphere	....
2	Company	....
3	Mechanic	....
4	Elephant	....
5	Deer	....

التدريب – IV
Translate the Following Words in English

English	Arabic	Roman	S.No
....	جزيرة	Jazeerah	1
....	رطوبة	Rutoobah	2
....	ميكانكى	Mechaniki	3
....	أجف	Ajaf	4
....	جميلة	Jameelah	5